# Guide to Vegetarian Brighton

Compiled and Edited by Jo Lacey

© Viva! 1998

Published by Viva! 1998; registered charity 1037486

Compiled & Edited by: Jo Lacey
Managing Editor: Juliet Gellatley
Assistant Editor: Graeme Wotherspoon

ISBN 0 9532800 0 4

Printed on 100% recycled paper by St Richards Press, Chichester

Published by Viva!
12 Queen Square
Brighton
E Sussex
BN1 3FD

Tel: 01273 777688
Fax: 01273 776755
E mail: info@viva.org.uk
Web site: www.viva.org.uk

## ACKNOWLEDGEMENTS

Thank you Silabhadra for designing the front cover image. Thanks to Greg
Walker for the veggiecons, original layout and help hotline! G Scene
generously let us use their map - much appreciated.
Cheers Graeme for all your help.
Thanks to Juliet for your editing, ideas and encouragement.

## Other publications by Viva!

The Silent Ark
A Chilling Expose of Meat - The Global Killer
by Juliet Gellatley with Tony Wardle

The Livewire Guide to Going, Being
and Staying Veggie
by Juliet Gellatley

Food for Life Video

Viva! Vegetarian and Vegan Guide
to the Lake District 1998-99
Edited by Kate Fowler

The L-Plate Vegetarian

The L-Plate Vegan

Viva! Guides to the Vegetarian/Vegan Issues

For further information, contact:
Viva!, 12 Queen Square
Brighton BN1 3FD
Tel: 01273 777688

## Comings and Goings
## Update Spring 2000

☺ **Infinity Foods Cooperative** has opened a cafe
(all vegetarian and vegan) on Gardner Street,
in the North Laine

☺ Viva! welcomes **Lush** - fabulously fresh body
treats at 41 East Street

☹ **The Burlington** (p. 106) now has a meat
menu with a few veggie options

☺ **Frogans** (p.109) has gone - but will re-open
somewhere else - watch this space!

☺ **Evolution** (p.116) has moved from North
Street to Bond Street (just around the corner)

☺ **The Waffle House** (p. 96) has gone and
been replaced by **Cafe Pasta**

☺ **Surfers Paradise** (p. 57) is now **Riki Tik**
serving organic and freerange food with lots
of veggie options and a fresh juice menu

☺ **Krakatoa** is a new Oriental restaurant offering a
great range of vegetarian and vegan cuisine -
find them at 7 Pool Valley (near the bus station)

☺ If you're in Horsham try **East Mews
Vegetarian Restaurant**, Tel: 01403 271125

☺ If your in Lewes check out **The Snowdrop Inn**,
Tel: 01273 471018

# CONTENTS

# Welcome to the Veggie Capital of Europe!

Brighton is a seductive place - according to its reputation. And it's all the fault of Prince George, the Prince Regent, later to become George IV. In 1787 he started work on the Royal Pavilion, the most bizarre, spectacular, fantastic, indulgent and eye popping weekend retreat ever conceived - a place where he could escape London and entertain his many 'friends'. He began a trend and people have been escaping to Brighton from London, Birmingham, and Newcastle ever since - and many of them never leave. In that sense the town is incredibly seductive; in fact you get free membership of Viva! if you can find anyone with a Sussex accent.

Brighton is a place of contrasts. It probably has more body piercings than anywhere else in Britain and, because of its conference facilities, more grey suits. The number of Big Issue sellers is matched only by the tally of antique shops and candy floss is consumed as gratefully as culture. There's reputedly a pub for every day of the year, all kinds of live music on most nights of the week and a club scene that ranks amongst the best. And there's some pretty spectacular churches too, so I'm told.

Wherever you go in the world people have heard of Brighton and frequently have named one of their own towns after it. So what is it that defines Brighton? I doubt if it's solely its wonderful Regency architecture and historic buildings such as Preston Manor or Siegfried Sassoon's mausoleum - now a pub. It's unlikely to be just its two piers, Palace and the beautiful West, at last to be rescued from its sad and desolate state. And, of course, when the town transforms itself in May with the biggest performance festival in England, something very special happens to it.

The uniquely narrow passageways - inviting, flint-walled 'twittens' - that make up the Lanes may also play a part in the enigma but then so do the North Laines with their individual shops, dreadlocks and sub culture. The Brighton of day trippers, seaside jollities, rock and over indulgence seems to exist separately and apart from the rest of the town yet must be an essential part of it. Even the markets - Sunday at the marina and station, Saturday in Upper Gardner Street - have the stamp of individuality about them. Where else could you sell a useless electric plug, last year's diary or a Sarajevo train time table written in Serbo Croat? But on its own, not enough.

A clue comes when people talk about Brighton. Everyone likes it. Those who live here, when they tell you where they come from, say the name with relish, rolling their tongue around it knowing that the response is never negative. They assume you know it, they expect you to like it, they anticipate you will be envious of their being a resident. I think it's called pride.

There are a huge number of young people in the town but barely a yuppie to be seen - nor a dinky, a post modernist, a self-motivating consumerist or whatever the current expression is. And that's particularly nice! In fact, many people come to Brighton because of that. They come in pursuit of individual fulfilment, whether it's tai chi, aromatherapy, to write a novel, paint a picture or blow a tune; and they drop into a community with a hugely strong anarchistic streak running through it - and they simply blend in. You can be whatever you want to be in Brighton. And now I think we're getting to the crux of it.

As long as living memory can recall, Brighton has been 'alternative' in the true sense. It has been a magnet to those who have rejected mainstream thinking, who can resist the siren call of uniformity, who think for themselves. And, of course, part of thinking is a rejection of the nastier bits of life such as killing animals needlessly.
Vegetarianism in Brighton is now part of the mainstream and is growing rapidly. Nowhere in Britain - in Europe - has such an extraordinary choice of dedicated veggie and vegan eating places or restaurants offering a great non-meat choice. And, of course, it is home to the wonderfully dynamic and effective vegetarian and vegan charity - Viva!.

As always, Brighton is ahead of the times. It is showing the way to an essential, compassionate, cruelty-free future and it's this, combined with its architectural beauty, its kiss-me-quick, self-indulgent, knocker-boy, 'got any loose change', thespian lovey, thriving, kaleidoscopic jumble of humanity that really marks it out as somewhere special. And I love it! So will you.

Tony Wardle

*Tony Wardle is a journalist, writer and TV producer and actively involved in Viva!'s work.*

# Key

(F) .................... Free-range eggs

.................... Veggie Cheese

.................... Table Service

.................... Counter Service

.................... Take Away

.................... Delivery

.................... All You Can Eat

.................... Special Diets Catered For

.................... Wine Available

.................... Veggie/Vegan Wine Available

.................... Bring Your Own

.................... Smoking Allowed

.................... Wheelchair Access

.................... Music

................ **Accept Cheques**

..................... **Accept Credit Cards**

(V)........................ **Vegan**

# Map Key

## Vegetarian Restaurants

The following are restaurants and pubs which are 100% vegetarian and shown on the map on pages 12 - 13:

❶ ........................ Bombay Aloo: page 79
❷ ........................ The Burlington: 106
❸ ........................ Food For Friends: 85
❹ ........................ Frogans: 109
❺ ........................ The George: 62
❻ ........................ The New Kensington: 54
❼ ........................ Seasons of Lewes: 124
❼ᵇ ........................ Seasons Wholefood Restaurant: 127
❽ ........................ The Sanctuary: 112
❾ ........................ Terre a Terre: 92
❿ ........................ Trogs: 45
⓫ ........................ The Vegetarian & Vegan
Sandwich Shop: 67
⓬ ........................ Wai Kika Moo Kau: 67


**P**........................ Parking
i........................ Tourist Information

# Grab 'n' Go...Veggie

**Save £5....Save £5....Save £5....Save £5....Save £5....**

The Silent Ark, Green Gastronomy & The Food For Life Video can all be yours for **£19.99** (+£2 p&p). Just fill in the form below and return to **Viva!**, 12 Queen Square, Brighton BN1 3FD.

**The Silent Ark**. Juliet Gellatley with Tony Wardle £6.99. Juliet's hard-hitting personal story is riveting, bold and persuasive. Classic book on all the vegetarian issues. Read it and never again be short of ammunition!

**Food for Life Video** £6.99 VHS 24mins. Brilliant and totally absorbing. Explores vegetarian/vegan issues - health; the animals; the environment and the developing world.

**Green Gastronomy**. Colin Spencer £9.99. Excellent, modern, delicious vegan cookbook. Imaginative & easy, a pleasure to use.

Yes! send me a **Grab and Go... Veggie** pack. I enclose £19.99 + £2 p&p (cheques payable to Viva!)

Name:_____

Address:_____

_____

Postcode:_____

to Viva!, 12 Queen Square, Brighton BN1 3FD

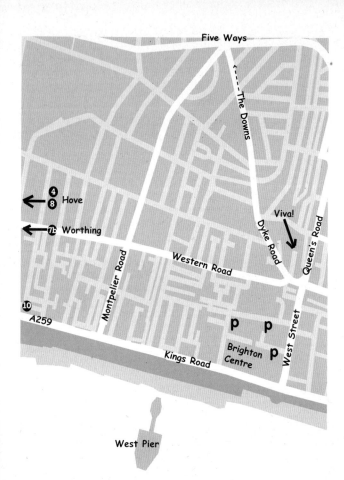

Five Ways

The Downs

Hove

Worthing

Viva!

Dyke Road

Queen's Road

Western Road

Montpelier Road

A259

Kings Road

West Street

Brighton Centre

West Pier

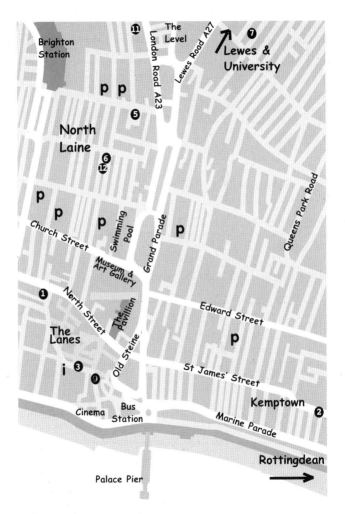

# PROVAMEL

## *Dairy free alternatives*

With Provamel's range of soya milks, desserts, flavoured drinks, creams and yoghurts there is no reason why anyone on a dairy-free diet has to miss out on choice or taste. As well as being dairy-free, all our products are low in fat, free of cholesterol, gluten free and many contain added calcium.

Provamel Yofu boasts all the many benefits you would normally associate with soya products yet has all the taste of a dairy yoghurt.

With a choice of black cherry and vanilla or peach and strawberry, Provamel Yofu makes cutting down on dairy products something to look forward to.

As versatile as their equivalent dairy products, the Provamel range can be found in selected supermarkets, Holland & Barrett and virtually all health foodshops.

For a free sample of Soya Milk and more information on soya products in general, please contact:-

Provamel - VIVA, Ashley House, 86-94 High Street, Hounslow, TW3 1NH.

# HOTELS

## Bannings Guest House

14 Upper Rock Gardens
Brighton          Tel: 01273 681403

**Bed & Breakfast**
**Price:** £18 - £22

**Veggie Breakfast:** Vegetarian Sausage, Hash Brown, Tomato, Mushroom and Scrambled Eggs.
**Vegan Breakfast:** As above with Beans instead of Eggs. Soya and Wheat Milk are available.
**Number of rooms:** 6
**En suite:** Some
**Views:** No views
This gay establishment offers a great vegan brekkie. Sorry guys, it's gals only at the weekends.

## Berkeley House Hotel

2 Albion Street
Lewes          Tel: 01273 476057

**Bed & Breakfast**
**Price:** £37.50 - £65

**Veggie Breakfast:** Cereals, Fruit Juices, Fresh Fruit, Toast, Eggs, Grilled Tomatoes & Baked Beans.
**Vegan Breakfast:** As above (without the Eggs). Soya-Milk and Soya Margarine are available.
**Number of rooms:** 5
**En suite:** Yes
**Views:** The top room has views across Lewes to the Downs. Two rooms look out across the garden and two look across the street.

*to Vegetarian Brighton*

Berkeley House is a Georgian town house in a quiet street in the centre of Lewes. Booking is advisable but there is a charge.

## Boydens

27 St James' Avenue
Brighton            Tel: 01273 601914  Fax: 01273 681133

**Bed & Breakfast**
**Price:** From £19 per person per night

**Veggie Breakfast:** Omlettes or Scrambled Eggs or Eggs, Tomatoes, Mushrooms, Fried Potatoes and Baked Beans
**Vegan Breakfast:** As above without the Eggs
**Number of rooms:** 6            **En suite:** Some - most with showers
**Views:** Victorian Terrace with a tree-lined street. Comfortable, clean and cosy with TV's and Tea and Coffee facilities in every room.

## Brighton Backpackers

75-76 Middle Street
Brighton
BN1 1AL            Tel: 01273 777717  Fax: 01273 887778
backpackers@fastnet.co.uk

**Beds and Self-catering Facilities**
**Price:** £9 - £10 in a dormitory or £25 for a double room.

**En suite:** In double rooms only. **Views:** Sea view with double rooms
A fun packed crazy place for international travellers and students, located in the centre of town with a relaxed and friendly atmosphere (no curfew). Internally it has painted murals and cartoon characters throughout. There are social areas with good hi-fi, satellite television, pool table and even music while you shower. Choose from staying in a dormitory or double room with a sea view and get cheap rates for water sports, roller-blading and bike hire.

# Dudley House

10 Madeira Place
Brighton
BN2 1TN          Tel: 01273 676794

### Bed & Breakfast
**Price:** £16 - £25 per person per night

**Veggie Breakfast:** Orange Juice, Cereal, Veggie Sausage, Egg, Tomato, Mushrooms, Beans & Toast.
**Vegan Breakfast:** As above with no Eggs (Soya Milk available).
**Number of rooms:** 6          **En suite:** 3
**Views:** En suite rooms have a sea view.
A central seafront location is the setting for this B&B, its also very reasonable.

# Friese Green

20 Middle Street
Brighton
BN1 1AL          Tel: 01273 747551
www.pdn.co.uk/friese-green

### Bed & Self Catering Facilities
**Price:** £9 -£10 for a bed in a dormitory or £12.50 for a small room.

**Number of rooms:** 50          **En suite:** yes
Friese Green is situated between the two piers in the Lanes, just 30 seconds away from the beach. The house has a friendly relaxed atmosphere, central heating, showers and baths.
There is a kitchen and a dining area, a TV room, a pool table and a cinema. Friese Green welcomes groups, teams, travellers, students and couples. Open 24 hours a day. Groups need to book 2-3 weeks in advance.

# Fyfield House Hotel

26 New Steine
Brighton
BN2 1PD          Tel: 01273 602770  Fax: 01273 602770
Fyfield@aol.com

**Bed & Breakfast with dinner on request**
**Price:** £16 - £30 per person per night

**Veggie Breakfast:** Grapefruit, Cereal, Yoghurt, Fruit, Toast, Egg, Tomatoes, Mushrooms, Beans, Hash Browns & Veggie Sausage (home-made)
**Vegan Breakfast:** As above (without the Yoghurt and Eggs) with Scrambled Tofu available
**Number of rooms:** 9          **En suite:** 6
**Views:** Views of the sea and gardens.
Fyfield House is a private hotel claiming to be a home from home. The hotel is two minutes away from the sea front and a pleasant stroll away from shops, theatres, pubs and clubs. Most of the rooms are en suite and one of the rooms has a four-poster bed. Peter and Anne are willing to cater for vegetarians and vegans, just let them know in advance what your needs are and they'll do their best to meet them.

# Genevieve Hotel

18 Madeira Place
Brighton
BN2 1TN          Tel: 01273 681653  Fax: 01273 681653

**Bed & Breakfast**
**Cost:** £20 - £25 per person per night

**Veggie Breakfast:** Continental - Croissant & Cereals
**Number of rooms:** 14          **En suite:** Yes
Just a one minute walk away from the seafront and the Palace Pier.

# The Granville

**124 Kings Road**
**Brighton**      Tel: 01273 326302  Fax: 01273 728294
**granville@brighton.co.uk**

**Hotel - Bed & Breakfast or Full Board**
**Price:** Between £49 (Single B&B) & £85 (Double)

**Veggie Breakfast:** Full Vegetarian Breakfast - Veggie Sausage, Veggie Bacon etc.
**Vegan Breakfast:** Vegan Sausage, Scrambled Tofu, Mushrooms, Fruit, Cereals etc.
**Rooms:** 24      **En suite:** All
**Views:** Rooms are individually designed and most have a view of Brighton seafront. A real veggie and vegan treat - you'll be well catered for at this hotel especially with Trogs restaurant attached - you don't even need to go outside. Trogs Restaurant has exquisite 100% vegetarian and mostly organic menu. The vegan options are excellent. See page 45-46.

# Grapevine

**29-30 North Road**
**Brighton**
**BN1 1YB**      Tel: 01273 681361
**Bed & Breakfast**
**Price:** £14.50 per person per night

**Veggie Breakfast:** Veggie Sausage, Fried Egg, Mushrooms, Fresh-fried Tomatoes, Beans, Toast or Bread 'n' Butter, Tea, Coffee or Cappuccino.
**Number of rooms:** 7      **Ensuite:** None
**Views:** Street.
Located on a North Laine main road. The cafe attached is very veggie friendly and does good food, but the B&B facilities are basic.

# Gullivers Guest House

10 New Steine
Brighton
BN2 1PB          Tel: 01273 695415

**Bed & Breakfast**
**Price:** £20 (single) & £38 - £48 (double)

**Veggie Breakfast:** Full English (with Linda McCartney Sausages)
**Vegan Breakfast:** Continental
**Number of rooms:** 8
**En suite:** Mostly     **Views:** Some rooms have a sea view.
Central and very near the seafront and the Palace Pier.

# Harvey's Guest House

1 Broad Street
Brighton
BN2 1TJ          Tel: 01273 699227

**Quality Bed & Breakfast**
**Price:** £15 - £25 per person per night

**Veggie Breakfast:** Eggs, Beans & Tomatoes
**Vegan Breakfast:** Vegan Sausages, Tomatoes & Beans (Soya Milk available)
**Number of rooms:** 8          **Ensuite:** 5
**Views:** Sea views
Very reasonable and flexible with some beautiful sea views thrown in.

# Hotel Seafield

Seafield Road
Hove
BN3 2TP          Tel: 01273 735912  Fax: 01273 323525

**Bed & Breakfast** (evening meal if required)
**Price:** Start at £25 per person per night or £35 for a single room

**Veggie Breakfast:** Scrambled Eggs, Tomatoes, Mushrooms & Potato Waffles
**Vegan Breakfast:** Tomatoes, Mushrooms, Potato Waffles & Baked Beans
**Number of rooms:** 14          **En suite:** 12
Just on the edge of the main shopping centre and close to the King Alfred Leisure Centre and the seafront.

# Kingsway Hotel

2 St Aubyns
Hove
BN3 2TB          Tel: 01273 722068  Fax: 01273 778409

**Bed & Breakfast**
**Price:** £22 - £65 per person per night

**Veggie Breakfast:** Poached Eggs, Scrambled Eggs on Toast, Veggie Sausages
**Vegan Breakfast:** Can accomodate vegans with prior notice
**Number of rooms:** 20          **Ensuite:** 8
**Views:** Sea views
Near the seafront in Hove and very near to the King Alfred Leisure Centre, for a slightly quieter time than the centre B&Bs.

## Palm Court

371 Kingsway
Hove
BN3 4QD          Tel: 01273 417821  Fax: 01273 417821

**Bed & Breakfast**
**Price:** from £15 per person per night

**Veggie Breakfast:** Eggs, Beans, Tomatoes, Mushrooms & Toast or Cheese on Toast
**Vegan Breakfast:** Beans, Tomatoes & Mushrooms on Toast
**Number of rooms:** 5          **En suite:** None
**Views:** 2 rooms have sea views
Open all year round 24 hours a day. Not very central, but buses are frequent and cheap into town.

## Paskins Town House

19 Charlotte Street
Brighton
BN2 1AG          Tel: 01273 601203  Fax: 01273 621973
welcome@paskins.co.uk

**Bed & Breakfast**
**Price:** Start at £20

**Veggie Breakfast:**  Choice of 3
**Vegan Breakfast:** Full Vegan Breakfast
**Number of rooms:** 20          **Ensuite:** Yes
**Views:** Like Paris!
Mostly organic produce used to create the full-on breakfasts. A few minutes walk from the Palace Pier and the Lanes and very near the sea front.

## Stakis Bedford & Stakis Metropole

Kings Road
Brighton       Tel: 01273 329744/775432
Fax: 01273 775877/207764   *Phone  0990 909090 to book*

**Bed & Breakfast or Full Board (Four Star)**
**Price:** £49.50 per person per night

**Veggie Breakfast:** Buffet Breakfast - Minimum 12 hot items and 8 cold items
**Vegan Breakfast:** As above - Soya Milk available
**Number of rooms:** 328        **En suite:** All rooms
**Views:** Some rooms have sea views, others of the hotel roof.
These two hotels are situated a mere 200 yards apart along the seafront and are central. Both are magnificent, glamorous and suitable for a very special occasion. The Metropole is a major function venue in the UK. It has a classy restaurant which is popular with guests and the public alike. It is large, bright and overlooks the sea - a good place for a celebration. The vegetarian options are imaginative and high quality. If you're a vegan let them know before you go and they'll give you plenty to choose from. The dishes are a la carte for example - Wild Mushroom Stroganoff in Filo Pastry, Sesame, Herb & Wild Rice Tofu Burgers (V), Char-grilled Aubergines with Vegetable Parcels, Vegetable Strudel on a Spring Onion & Corriander Creme. 3 Course menu £17.95

## The Twenty One Hotel

21 Charlotte Street
Marine Parade
Brighton
BN2 1AG        Tel: 01273 686450  Fax: 01273 695560
http:www.chelsoft.demon.co.uk/21.htm

**Bed & Breakfast**
**Price:** £35 - £50

**Veggie Breakfast:** Full Vegetarian Breakfast
**Vegan Breakfast:** Scrambled Eggless on Toast with Mushrooms or Vegan Muesli
**Number of rooms:** 8       **En suite:** Yes
**Views:** Three with sea views.
Located in a quiet side street, just a few steps from the beach, the Twenty One is an early Victorian town house. They offer many special breaks, such as a trip to France, or a Christmas treat. Vegetarians and vegans are well catered for with a separate menu. The Twenty One claims to be the best Bed & Breakfast in Brighton. It is well worth visiting their website for a look at the individually designed rooms, some with four-poster beds.

# Willow Guest House

37 Russell Square
Brighton
BN1 2EF       Tel: 01273 326129

**Bed & Breakfast**
**Price:** From £15 per person per night

**Veggie Breakfast:** Vegetarian English Breakfast with Vegetarian Sausage or Scrambled Egg on Toast/Continental Style
**Number of rooms:** 10       **En suite:** 3
**Views:** Front views over Russell Square Gardens
Situated between the main shopping area and the seafront. A recently refurbished Regency building offers a cosy retreat.

*Hundred metres from the beach and an easy walk to all major attractions*
*All rooms fully en suite and exquisitely furnished*
*Dive into a delicious breakfast catering for
Vegans and Vegetarians*
*Up to 30% discounts available -
Call us now for the best price

**The Twenty One**        Tel: 01273 686450/681617
**21 Charlotte Street**    Fax: 01273 695560/681617
**Brighton**               e-mail: the 21@pavillion.co.uk
**BN2 1AG**

*www.chelsoft.demon.co.uk/21.htm*

### Akash Tandoori (Restaurant)

**6 Preston Street**
**Brighton**          01273 324494

**Type of Cuisine:** Indian

**Breakdown:** (out of over 100 dishes) **Vegetarian:** 40%; **Vegan:** 0%

A wide selection of vegetable curries on offer - so if curry is what does it for you then go to Akash. Choose from hot, hotter or stupidly hot!

Vegetable Bhoona - £3.65, Vegetable Vindaloo - £3.65, Dall Soup - £1.95, Vegetable Samosa - £2.55, Mushroom Curry - £3.35, Pilaw Rice - £1.55, Aloo Gobi Balti - £5.50, Chana Gobi Balti - £5.50
*Opening Hours*
*Monday - Saturday: Noon - 3pm & 6pm - Midnight*
*Sunday: Noon - Midnight*
**Additional**
Service is not included and booking is only necessary on weekends.

### Arcade Coffee House (Cafe)

**15b Imperial Arcade**
**Brighton**          01273 326600
**Type of Cuisine:** Snacks and Cakes

**Breakdown:** (out of 20 dishes) **Vegetarian:** 20%; **Vegan:** 0%

The Arcade Coffee House serves good fresh coffee - the smell of which always adds to the atmosphere of a place. Unimaginative vegetarian choices.
*Opening Times*
*Monday - Saturday: 8am - 5.30pm*
**Additional**
**Music:** Old Time Jazz music
**Service:** No charge
**Booking:** Not necessary

# Bombay Indian Cuisine (Restaurant)

**85-87 Preston Street**
**Brighton          01273 732199**

**Type of Cuisine:** Indian/English

**Breakdown:** (out of over 100 dishes) **Vegetarian:** 25%; **Vegan:** 0%

The Bombay is fully air conditioned so even if your tonsils are screaming you can keep your cool. Their wide variety of dishes from Vegetable Bhoona to Sag Aloo are selected from all regions of India to spice up your life.

Vegetable Biriany - £5.25, Sag Bhajee - £2.25, Navrattan Korma (mild curry with yoghurt & cream) - £4.10, Sag Aloo (spinach & potato) - £2.45, Special Fried Rice - £2.25
*Opening Times*
*Monday - Saturday: Noon - 2.30pm & 6pm - Midnight*
*Sunday: Noon - Midnight*

## Bombay Mix (Restaurant)
104 Western Road
Brighton          01273 722280

**Type of Cuisine:** Indian Buffet

**Breakdown:** (out of 15 dishes) **Vegetarian:** 90%; **Vegan:** 40%

Bombay Mix is the almost-veggie brother of Bombay Aloo which has been a popular Indian vegetarian restaurant in Brighton for a long time. It has the same 'all you can eat' policy and there's a good spicy selection on offer. Most of the dishes could set your soul on fire and are very tasty. Well worth a try.

All You Can Eat from the Indian Buffet  - £4.50
*Opening Hours*
*Every day: Noon - 11pm*
**Additional**
**Service:** No charge       **Booking:** Not necessary


## Bon Appetit (Cafe)
48 West Street
Brighton          01273 732832

**Type of Cuisine:** Hot Snacks

**Breakdown:** (out of 50 dishes) **Vegetarian:** 20%; **Vegan:** 0%

Veggie Burgers, Chips, Omelettes and Pizzas are on the menu at Bon Appetit. So if that's what you fancy its a good place to go.

Veggie Breakfast (2 veggie sausages, 2 eggs, beans, mushrooms,

chips & tomatoes with tea/coffee) - £3.95, Garlic Bread - £1.50,
Vegetarian Pizza - £5, Veggie Burgers - £3.20-£3.85
*Opening Hours*
*Sunday - Thursday: Noon - 10pm    Friday - Saturday: Noon - 2am*

## Brighton Bystander (Cafe)
**1 Terminus Road**
**Brighton**      **01273 329364**

**Type of Cuisine:** Breakfasts and Hot Snacks

**Breakdown:** (out of 200 dishes) **Vegetarian:** 40%; **Vegan:** 10%

The Bystanders are Brighton's very own greasy spoons. They have a
good range of vegetarian and vegan dishes - both clearly labelled.

Veggie Gut Buster (veggie burger, veggie sausage, egg, beans,
tomato, mushrooms & chips) - £4.55,  Vegan Breakfast - £3.25
*Opening Hours*
*Every day: 8am - 12.30am*

## Clock Tower Cafe

**10 Dyke Road**
**Brighton**                **01273 298085**
**Type of Cuisine:** Greasy spoon par excellence

**Breakdown:** (out of 100 dishes) **Vegetarian:** 25%; **Vegan:** 25%

Tiny caff and grumpy owner - but extraordinary choice and value!

Veggie 'Steak' Pie, 3 Veg & Gravy - £2.20, Veggie mince & Onion
Pie, Chips & Peas - £2.20
*Opening Hours*    *Monday - Friday: Early - 3pm*

## C & H Fabrics Pavilion Coffee Shop (Cafe)

**179 Western Road**
**Brighton**          **01273 321671**

**Type of Cuisine:** Snacks and hot food

**Breakdown:** (out of 50 dishes) **Vegetarian:** 50%; **Vegan:** 0%

In a cosy corner of the haberdashery department, this Coffee Shop has a wide range of pastries and cakes, labelled 'V' for veggie.

Vegetarian Soup - £1.50, Carrot Cake - £1
*Opening Hours          Monday - Saturday: 9am - 5pm*

## Dig in the Ribs Ltd (Restaurant)

**47 Preston Street**
**Brighton**          **01273 325275**

**Type of Cuisine:** Mexican

**Breakdown:** (out of 35 dishes) **Vegetarian:** 30%; **Vegan:** 0%

I was pleasantly surprised to find a selection of vegetarian dishes at a place called Dig in the Ribs - I thought it would be cow pie all round! In fact the dishes are tasty and the restaurant has a spacious, new-style Mexican theme. Give it a go Gringo!

Chimichanga (large crisp burrito topped with guacamole, salsa & sour cream) - £8.95, Nachos with Sour Cream & Guacamole - £3.25, Sunshine Salad (star fruit, kiwi, melon, mango, pineapple and orange on a garden salad with pine kernels & cashews) - £6.95
*Opening Hours  Monday - Saturday: Noon - 11pm  Sunday: Noon - 10.30pm*

## Havana (Restaurant)

32 Duke Street
Brighton          01273 773388

**Type of Cuisine:** Modern Gourmet

**Breakdown:** (out of 21 dishes) **Vegetarian:** 10%; **Vegan:** 5%

From the outside Havana looks quite small, but once you're in through the doors it opens out into palatial splendour. A grand piano, large plants and a waterfall set the scene for culinary delights. Exquisite cuisine is the order of the day at Havana for vegetarians. There's not much choice - but what there is will certainly satisfy.

Artichoke and Hazelnut Cannelloni, Herb Yoghurt & Oil Leaves - £11.95, Char Grilled Cep Tortilla, Roasted Asparagus & Eggplant with Oven Dried Tomato Oil (V) - £7.50, Calamato & Plum Tomato Bruschetta - £3.95
*Opening Hours*
*Every day: 10am - 11pm*
**Additional**
**Music:** Live Jazz on Saturday nights
**Service:** Not included   **Booking:** Necessary, esp. on weekends


## Jason's (Take-Away)

50 North Street
Brighton          01273 220254

**Type of Cuisine:** Sandwiches and Pastries

**Breakdown:** (out of 100 dishes) **Vegetarian:** 30%; **Vegan:** 10%

Jason's is just down the road from the Viva! offices, so we often have smelly breath from our constant supply of vegan humous and salad sarnies!! They can make sandwiches to order and serve fresh soup during the winter months. There are lots of veggie pasties and vegan samosas and bhajis.

Spicy Vegetarian Roll - 80p, Garlic & Mushroom Pasty - £1.10, Humous & Salad Focaccia (V) - £1.60, Cheese & Leek Pasty - £1.10, Ricotta, Spinach, Lentil & Tomato Parcel - £1.10, Homity Pie - £1.10, Various Soups - £1
*Opening Hours*
*Monday - Saturday: 7am - 6.30pm    Sunday: 11am - 6pm*

## Kambi's (Restaurant)
**170 Western Road**
**Brighton        01273 327934**

**Type of Cuisine:** Lebanese

**Breakdown:** (out of 60 dishes) **Vegetarian:** 50%; **Vegan:** 15%

Loads of vegetarian options to eat in or take out. The falafel and humous in pitta bread with tahini sauce is a delicious take-away. Look out for the prawn and vegetable curry in the vegetarian main course section - I think it's a red herring!!

Warakinab (Vine Leaves Stuffed with Rice, Tomato, Herbs & Spices) (V) - £2.50, Moussaka Batinjan (fried aubergine with chickpeas, tomatoes & spices) - £2.50, Sambousak (pastry filled with cheese, onion & pine nuts) - £2.75
*Opening Hours*
*Monday - Saturday: Noon - Midnight   Sunday: Noon - 11.30pm*

## Mamma Mia (Restaurant)

68 Preston Street
Brighton          01273 326823

**Type of Cuisine:** Italian

**Breakdown:** (out of 86 dishes) **Vegetarian:** 20%; **Vegan:** 0%

Mamma Mia is an authentic Italian restaurant offering pizza and pasta with rich tangy sauces.

Cannelloni Mamma Mia - £4.50/£5.50
*Opening Hours*
*Everyday: Noon - 2 & 6pm - 11.30pm*
**Additional**
**Service:** 10% service charge
**Booking:** Necessary on weekends

## Oasis (Sandwich Bar)

4 Air Street
Brighton

**Type of Cuisine:** Sandwiches & hot food

**Breakdown:** (out of 40 dishes) **Vegetarian:** 30%; **Vegan:** 2%

Typical sandwich bar but with more choice than most.
Veggie Sausage Sandwich - £1.55 or Humous Baguette (V) - £1.35, Various Pasties

*Opening Hours*
*Monday - Saturday: 7.30am - 4pm*

# Parasol Coffee House (Cafe)

3 Cranbourne Street
Brighton          01273 735284

**Type of Cuisine:** Snacks and Cakes

**Breakdown:** (out of 20 dishes) **Vegetarian:** 20%; **Vegan:** 0%

Unimaginative veggie options - but a good range of ice cream sundaes, one of which could easily be adapted for vegans. Nice place for a coffee.

Toasted Cheese & Onion Sandwich - £2.15, Macaroni Cheese - £3.30, Poached Egg or Beans on Toast - £1.20, Cheese Sandwich - £1.90, Ice Cream Sundaes - £2.95 - £3.85
*Opening Hours*
*Monday - Saturday: 8am - 5.30pm     Sunday: 11.30pm - 5pm*

**Additional**
**Music:** Old Time Jazz music          **Booking:** Not necessary

# Paris Texas American Bistro (Restaurant)

128 Western Road
Brighton          01273 747111
usabistro@aol.com

**Type of Cuisine:** Tex-Mex

**Breakdown:** (out of 50 dishes) **Vegetarian:** 35%; **Vegan:** 25%

Live life to the full American Style at Paris Texas where big portions and lots of flavour are the key to success. Vegetarians and vegans are well catered for, choose from tortillas, fajitas or chimichanga and enjoy the taste of America.

Deep-Fried Potato Skins with sour cream, salsa and guacomole - £2.75, Courgette, Aubergine and Tomato Fajitas - £8.95, Spicy Vegetable Burrito and Chimichanga - £7.25, Californian Salad (greens topped with avocado, nuts, olives, raisins & orange) - £7.25

*Opening Hours*
*Sunday - Thursday: 11am - 10pm*     *Friday & Saturday: 11am - 11pm*

**Additional**
**Music:** Cajun, 70's, 80's and Blues
**Service:** Discretionary/Charge of 10% for 8 or more people
**Booking:** Yes - especially Friday and Saturday

## Pierre Victoire (Restaurant)

**5 Cranbourne Street**
**Brighton**            **01273 205605**

**Type of Cuisine:** French

**Breakdown:** (out of 10-20 dishes) **Vegetarian:** 20%; **Vegan:** 0%

Have special theme nights and cater for large parties with any dietary needs. The chef is happy to adapt the menu to your requirements with prior warning. There is always at least one vegetarian option on the menu.

Pasta with Wild Mushrooms - £5, A Tian of Aubergine with Goats Cheese, Ratatouille & Red Pepper Oil - £5, Tossed Fresh Pasta with Wild Mushrooms, Garlic & Fresh Parmesan Cheese - £5
*Opening Hours*
*Sunday & Monday: Noon - 3pm*
*Tuesday - Saturday: Noon - 3pm & 6pm - 11pm*
**Additional**
**Service:** No charge     **Booking:** Not necessary

## Pizza Hut (UK) Ltd (Restaurant)
81-82 Western Road
Brighton          01273 327991

**Type of Cuisine:** Pizza/Pasta

**Breakdown:** (out of 20 dishes) **Vegetarian:** 25%; **Vegan:** 0%

The cheese on the pizzas is vegetarian - hooray! However they don't offer any vegan dishes, apart from the salad bar of course.

Country Feast Pizza - £7.99, Vegetable Pasta Bake - £5.49,
Vegetarian Ultimo Pizza - £4.99/£7.59/£9.99, Garlic Bread - £1.69
*Opening Hours*
*Monday - Saturday: Noon -11pm    Sunday: Noon - 10pm*

**Additional**
**Music:** Various - popular and easy listening

## Prince of India (Restaurant)
17 Preston Street
Brighton          01273 323868

**Type of Cuisine:** Indian

**Breakdown:** (out of 150 dishes) **Vegetarian:** 10%; **Vegan:** 0%

The Princely dishes are specialities from all regions of India, they are highly nutritious and tasty with a subtle blend of herbs and spices. The food is freshly prepared every day.

# THE VIVA! WINE CLUB

**The Viva! Wine Club offers wines, spirits, ciders, beers and soft drinks guaranteed to be free from any animal ingredients. Our selection of more than 50 wines really does represent superb value and many are organic as well as being cruelty-free. Why not treat yourself? All orders are despatched without delay and often arrive within a week of us receiving the order.**

**Call Viva! for a free catalogue on 01273 777688.**

Mixed Vegetable Dupiaza - £2.55, Mixed Vegetable Bhoona - £2.55, Vegetable Vindaloo - £2.55, Spinach Bhajee - £1.75, Vegetable Balti - £4.95

*Opening Hours*
*Every day: 5pm - late*

# Sapporo Teppanyaki (Restaurant)
**38-40 Preston Street**
**Brighton**          **01273 730940/734862**

**Type of Cuisine:** Japanese

**Breakdown:** (out of 40 dishes) **Vegetarian:** 25%; **Vegan:** 10%

Lots of raw fish on the menu, but there is a set vegetarian menu for £15 which is unusual and tasty. Stylish, sparse decor with large communal seating.

Set meal - £15 including Cucumber Maki Roll, Fresh Egg Drop Soup, Mixed Vegetables in Batter, Fresh Saial, Fried Rice, Tofu, Onion, Mushrooms & Courgettes followed by Fresh Fruit
*Opening Times*
*Monday - Friday: Noon - 2.30pm & 6pm - 11pm*
*Saturday & Sunday: 11am - 11.30pm*

**Additional**
**Service:** 10% service added to the bill
**Booking:** Necessary on weekends

# The Bengal View (Restaurant)

**12 Preston Street**
**Brighton**          01273 778721/328662

**Type of Cuisine:** Tandoori & Balti

**Breakdown:** (out of 150 dishes) **Vegetarian:** 20%; **Vegan:** 0%

The Bengal View offers the best tradition of Bangladeshi and North India. They use no artificial additives in their dishes and have about 30 dishes which are vegetarian.

Vegetable Korma (mild with coconut) - £3.05, Vegetable Vindaloo - £2.75, Chana Sag (Spinach & Chick Peas) - £3.05, Mushroom Balti - £5.25, Sag Wall Dhall - £3.05, Bhindi Tomato Curry - £3.05

*Opening Hours*
*Every day: Noon - 2.30pm & 6pm - Midnight*
**Additional**
**Booking:** Necessary at weekends

# The Big Bite Centre (Take-Away)

**60 Preston Street**
**Brighton**          01273 737082

**Type of Cuisine:** Sandwiches and hot food

**Breakdown:** (out of 50 dishes) **Vegetarian:** 20%; **Vegan:** 0%

If you're not in the mood for cooking after a hard day - just chill out and the Big Bite Centre will deliver what you want. All products are prepared fresh daily and portions are larger than life.

Shepherd's Pie (with various toppings) - £2.95, Mushroom Bake - £3.25, Beano Pie - £1.10, Cheese & Onion Pie - £1.20, Aubergine Bake - £3.25, Veggie Bolognaise - £2.95

*Opening Hours*
*Sunday - Wednesday: Early - 1am*
*Thursday - Saturday: Early - 3am*

## Tsing Tao (Restaurant)

**33 Preston Street**
**Brighton**      **01273 202708**

**Type of Cuisine:** Oriental

**Breakdown:** (out of 200 dishes) **Vegetarian:** 10%; **Vegan:** 5%

Tsing Tao claims to be one of the finest Peking and Szechuan restaurants in Sussex with a wide range of dishes.

Deep Fried Vegetarian Bean Curd Roll (V) - £3, Sweet & Sour Baby Sweetcorn - £4, Hoi Choi - £3, Deep Fried Asparagus - £3, Sea Spice Mixed Vegetable & Beancurd - £4
*Opening Hours*
*Every day: Noon - Midnight*

## Viceroy Of India (Restaurant)

**13 Preston Street**
**Brighton**      **01273 324733**

**Type of Cuisine:** Tandoori

**Breakdown:** (out of 200 dishes) **Vegetarian:** 20%; **Vegan:** 0%

The Viceroy claims to provide Brighton's foremost authentic Indian cuisine in an elegant and exotic atmosphere. Vegans can sit this one out though.

Vegetable Ceylon - £2.55, Kulcha Nan - £1.55, Vegetable Pathia - £3.65, Nan Stuffed with Almonds & Sultanas - £1.55, Gobi Bhajee - £1.85, Sag Ponir - £1.85
*Opening Hours*
*Every day: Noon - 3pm & 6pm - Midnight*

**Additional**
**Service:** 10% service charge

# Woolworth's (Cafe)
**Western Road**
**Brighton**

**Type of Cuisine:** Snacks and hot food

**Breakdown:** (out of 50 dishes) **Vegetarian:** 30%; **Vegan:** 5%

One of the best bargains in town is breakfast in Woolies. Not the classiest location but who can complain at £1.75 for a choice of 8 cooked breakfast goodies.

Full Veggie Breakfast 8 items - £1.75 or 5 items - £1.30

You'll find Brighton's one & only
authentic bagel bakery/cafe
at the
'SUSSEX INNOVATION CENTRE'
Sussex University, Falmer
(just off the A27 to Lewes, on the
campus' Southern Ring Road)

Open Mon-Fri  8.30am ~ 3.30pm
*(Veggie breakfasts until 10.30am)*
☎ (01273) 704407

## The Bagelman (Take-Away)

Sussex Innovation Centre Science
Park Square
Falmer
Brighton          01273 704407

Bagels@Bagelman.co.uk

**Type of Cuisine:** Deli-Style Bagels

**Breakdown:** (out of 20ish dishes) **Vegetarian:** 75%; **Vegan:** 50%

Situated on the University campus The Bagelman is Brighton's one
and only authentic bagel bakery. Cooked on the premises, they are
absolutely delicious. The bagels are 100% animal-free (of course
the toppings may not be). You can have whatever you fancy in
your bagel (within reason)!

Between 8.30 and 10.30am: French Toast Bagel (fried bagel
quarters soaked in egg and milk served with maple syrup,
cinnamon and optional cream). Humous Salad Bagel (V) - £1.80
with Tabbouleh (V) - 80p

*Opening Hours*
*Monday - Friday: 8.30am - 3.30pm*

## The Cook & Fiddle (Restaurant)

183 Kings Road Arches
Brighton
BN1 1NB          01273 739530

**Type of Cuisine:** Fresh Fish & Veggie

**Breakdown:** (out of 15 dishes) **Vegetarian:** 50%; **Vegan:** 20%

As a seasonal seafront restaurant The Cook & Fiddle is open all days April to September and weekends from mid-October to Christmas. Main courses change each week and appear on the blackboards. The food here is home-made and most of the ingredients come from local farms that use traditional, non-intensive methods. Most of the menu is vegetarian and vegans are well catered for too.

Mediterranean Sunshine Salad (V) - £3.95, Vegetable Crepes with Seasonal Filling & Gratinated with Cheese Sauce - £3.50, Pasta with Wild Mushrooms - £4.95, Ice Cream Pancake with Fresh Fruit Coulis - £2.25

**Additional**
**Music:** Spanish guitar at the weekends
**Organic:** Organic flour, pasta and apple juice are used.
**Booking:** Necessary in the evenings

## The Plaza (Restaurant)

43 Kings Road
Brighton          01273 232222

**Type of Cuisine:** Various

**Breakdown:** (out of 18 dishes) **Vegetarian:** 20%; **Vegan:** 0%

The Plaza may look a bit pricey at first glance, but as well as your meal you get a beautiful sea view, live music and somewhere that's open until 2am. The live music includes soul on Tuesday, jazz and soul on Wednesday and Thursday, 60's, 70's, 80's & 90's on Friday with a touch of Latin music on Saturday - take your pick.

Oyster Shell Melon - £4.95, Crispy Crepe Parcels - £8.95, Stilton & Grape Choux - £4.95, Mushroom Roasted Peppers - £9.95
*Opening Hours*
*Monday - Saturday: 11am - 2am      Sunday: 11am - 1am*

**Additional**
**Music:** Live music Tuesday-Saturday
**Service:** 10% service charge      **Booking:** Necessary at weekends

## Trogs (Restaurant)

124 Kings Road
Brighton          01273 326302
granville@brighton.co.uk

**Type of Cuisine:** Vegetarian & Vegan

**Breakdown:** (out of 4 courses) **Vegetarian:** 100%; **Vegan:** 50%
Trogs, with its seafront location and glorious range of dishes, is

ideal for that special occasion. Trogs is 100% vegetarian with an extensive vegan menu which changes nearly every week. It is highly stylish with whitewash walls, modern sculptures and a very friendly, eccentric waiter who thinks the world is 'marvellous'!! Trogs Tavern is the adjoining bar which serves vegetarian bar food and plenty of vegan wines and beers to wash them down with. Or you can sit in the restaurant and enjoy the journey of four courses for £15.50.

Fan of Avocado with Walnut Vinaigrette (V), Roasted Tomato & Asparagus Tartlette with Chervil & White Wine Sauce(V), Spicey Peanut Satay Kebabs(V), Apple & Calvados Tartlette with Cinnamon Cream - £15.50 for four courses.
*Opening Hours*
*Every day: 6pm - 9.30pm*
**Additional**
**Organic:** Use organic wherever possible
**Alcohol:** 32 different wines and 20 different beers available
**Service:** 10% Service Charge

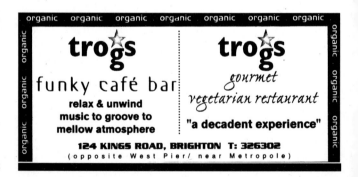

# NORTH LAINE

## Annie's Kitchen at The Great Eastern (Pub)
**103 Trafalgar Street**
**Brighton**      01273 685681

**Type of Cuisine:** Continental/Mexican

**Breakdown: Vegetarian:** 50%; **Vegan:** 0%

Annie's Kitchen provides a selection of freshly cooked vegetarian scrummies. The menu is half veggie - so always lots of choice. "Eat to your heart's content at the Great Eastern" say Cosmopolitan, we couldn't agree more! Disappointing that there's no options for vegans. Jazz, acoustic and indie tunes will keep your lug-holes happy while you cram it in!

Mushroom, Avocado & Brie melt on Pitta with salad - £4.50, Taco shells served with Vegetarian Chilli, Salsa, Sour Cream, Salad & Cheese - £4.75
*Opening Hours*
*Monday - Saturday: Noon - 11pm      Sunday: Noon - 10.30pm*

**Additional:**
**Music:** Jazz/acoustic and indie in the evening
**Booking:** Necessary

# Cafe Motu (Cafe)

6 Trafalgar Street
Brighton          01273 270895

**Type of Cuisine:** Various

**Breakdown:** (out of 10 dishes) **Vegetarian:** 10%; **Vegan:** 0%

The food is freshly cooked at Cafe Motu and out of the 9 dishes on the menu which changes regularly, there are one or two vegetarian options. The decor is cool and there's a good atmosphere.

Mushroom Casserole (with Cream, Brandy & Parsley) & Garlic Bread - £3.20, Herb Omelette with Tomato & Toast - £2.10
*Opening Hours*
Monday - Saturday: 9am - 6pm      Sunday: CLOSED
**Additional**
**Music:** Mellow jazz

# Cafe Tiffin (Cafe)

22 North Road
Brighton          01273 674209

**Type of Cuisine:** Mediterranean

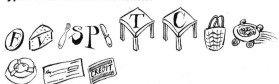

**Breakdown:** (out of 100 dishes) **Vegetarian:** 60%; **Vegan:** 40%

Cafe Tiffin is an extremely popular cafe in the North Laines. The food is very tasty and not expensive. The veggie options are easily identified on the blackboard and there are lots of them. There are vegan goodies too. Bustling at lunch times, but well worth the squeeze for nutritious and yummy nosh.

Mediterranean Roast Vegetable Cous Cous - £3.80, Black Eye Bean & Spinach Casserole (V) - £4

*Opening Hours*
*Monday - Saturday: 9am - 5pm*


## Capers (Cafe)
**27 Gardner Street**
**Brighton**          01273 675550

**Type of Cuisine:** All Day Breakfast and Hot Snacks

**Breakdown:** (out of 30 dishes) **Vegetarian:** 20%; **Vegan:** 0%

Choose from a veggie breakfast, sandwich or jacket potato if you fancy a snack or alternatively tuck into veggie bangers and mash.

Vegetarian Home-made Soup - £1.70, Veggie Bangers & Mash with Onion Gravy - £4.60, All-Day Veggie Breakfast - £3.90, Scrambled or Fried Eggs & Beans on Two Slices of Toast - £2.35

*Opening Hours*
*Monday - Friday: 9am - 6pm*          *Saturday: 9am - 5pm*

## Domino's Pizza (Take-Away)

**16-17 St George's Place**
**Brighton**          01273 675676

**Type of Cuisine:** Pizzas

**Breakdown:** (out of 70 dishes) **Vegetarian:** 50%; **Vegan:** 25%

Domino's Pizza will tailor make a pizza just for you. If you don't want cheese they can smother your pizza in garlic and stack up the toppings. And you can have your munchies delivered to your door.

Garlic Bread - £1.95, Vegetarian Supreme - £4.25 - £12.25 depending on size, Chocolate Mousse £1.50
*Opening Hours*
*Every Day: Noon - 10pm (carry out)/11pm (delivery)*

## Food for Thought (Cafe)

**16 Kensington Gardens**
**Brighton**          01273 674919

**Type of Cuisine:** Home-made Hot Snacks

**Breakdown:** (out of 50 dishes)  **Vegetarian:** 20%; **Vegan:** 0%

Food for Thought is a bright and fresh cafe with a good range of vegetarian dishes which are all home-made.

Nut Roast with Chips or Salad - £3.75, Potato, Cheese & Spinach Pie - £3.75, Pasta Bake - £3.75, Quiche - £3
*Opening Hours*
*Monday - Saturday: 8.30am - 5.30pm*

## Gardner Cafe (Cafe)

5 Gardner Street
Brighton

**Type of Cuisine:** Hot Snacks

**Breakdown:** (out of 75 dishes) **Vegetarian:** 10%; **Vegan:** 0%

The Gardner Cafe is a pleasant caf with a few traditional options.

Spinach & Onion Cheese Melt - £4, Mushroom & Cheese Melt - £4, Jacket Potato & Beans - £2.50, Veggie Breakfast - £3.25
*Opening Hours*
*Every day: 9.30am - 6.30pm*

## Hudson's (Cafe)

12 Sydney Street
Brighton                    **01273 671266**

**Type of Cuisine:** Hot Snacks & Sandwiches

**Breakdown:** (out of 50 dishes) **Vegetarian:** 10%; **Vegan:** 0%

Mr Hudson's calls itself a Diner rather than a Cafe, but it serves up the same old hot snacks and sandwiches with nothing original on offer for veggies. They do a good veggie breakfast though.

Veggie Sausage sandwich - £1.20, Omelettes, Toasted Sandwiches, Tomatoes on Toast - £1.60
*Opening Hours*
*Monday - Friday: 9am - 4.30pm      Saturday: 8.30am - 5pm*

# Now Wear This!

## ...T-shirts from Viva!

**For the full range, contact Viva! for our free Gifts For Life catalogue**

## Animal Power!

Animal Power rules OK with these cool V-neck T-shirts. State colour (black or white); and size (M/L) when ordering. **£9.99** (plus £2 p+p) from Viva!.

## Don't Mess with the Animals

Help the animals fight back with Viva!'s no-nonsense slogan on a stylish black T-shirt and swirly, multi-coloured background. State size XL/M when ordering.
**£9.99** (plus £2 p+p) from:
**Viva!, 12 Queen Square, Brighton BN1 3FD**

*(Make cheque payable to Viva!)*

Or pay by credit card on tel: 01273 777688

# Kensington Cafe (Cafe)

1A Kensington Gardens
Brighton      01273 570963

**Type of Cuisine:** Breakfasts & Hot Snacks

**Breakdown:** (out of 100 dishes) **Vegetarian:** 10%; **Vegan:** 5%

Up above the busy streets of Brighton is the Kensington Cafe. Chips with vegetarian gravy, chilli with rice, chips or nachos, veggie breakfasts - take your pick from the blackboards which cover most of the walls. The veggie sausage sandwiches are vegan and so is the chilli with nachos. Soya milk is available so treat yourself to a cup of tea to wash it down.

Veggie Breakfast - £3.35, Veggie Chilli with Nachos (V) - £3.95, Chips 'n' Gravy - £1.60, Vegetable Chilli with Rice or Chips - £3.45, Veggie Sausage Sandwich/Baguette (V) - £1.70, Nachos with Refried Beans - £3.95, Cakes, Muffins, Fruit Teas
*Opening Hours*
*Every day: 9.30am - 5.30pm*

# Mei-Mei Chinese Cuisine (Cafe)

11 York Place
Brighton      01273 695645

**Type of Cuisine:** Chinese & Baked Potatoes

**Breakdown:** (out of 100 dishes) **Vegetarian:** 10%; **Vegan:** 0%

The decor at Mei Mei is very basic, so if you'd rather eat in the comfort of your own home they do free delivery within 2 miles. The dishes on offer to vegetarians are vegetable based with a variation on the sauces - black bean, garlic or sweet & sour.

Vegetables in Sweet & Sour Sauce - £2.65, Vegetables in a Blackbean Sauce - £2.65, Mixed Vegetables in a Garlic Sauce - £2.60
*Opening Hours*
*Monday - Thursday: Noon - 2.30pm & 5.30pm - Midnight*
*Friday & Saturday: Noon - 2.30pm & 5.30pm -1am    Sunday: 5pm - Midnight*

## The New Kensington (Pub)  ❻
**13 Kensington Gardens**
**Brighton          01273 681907**

**Type of Cuisine:** Veggie & Vegan

**Breakdown:** (out of 30 dishes) **Vegetarian:** 100%; **Vegan:** 99%

99% vegan - amazing! The Workers co-operative is a new development in the Kenny and they're specialising in pies. The Sunday Roast (V) is totally divine.  The New Kensington is the ultimate alternative pub in the North Laines - dreadlocks not compulsory!

Tempeh, Corriander & Apricot Pie/Tofu, Mushroom & Red Wine Pie - served with Mash, Peas & Gravy (V) - £3.85, Daily Specials (always V) - eg Courgette Lasagne - £1.95, Burgers - Tempeh/Tofu with Salad in an Organic Wholemeal Bap (V) -  £1.95, Sunday Roast en Croute (with roast potatoes, roast parsnips, vegetables & gravy) (V) - £3.50
*Opening Hours*
*Monday - Saturday: 11.30am - 7pm     Sunday: 12.30pm - 4pm*

## Oriental Diner (Cafe/Restaurant)

18 York Place
Brighton          01273 888388

**Type of Cuisine:** Chinese and English

**Breakdown:** (out of 150 dishes) **Vegetarian:** 40%; **Vegan:** 20%

This is one of my favourites! You walk through the front part of the shop which is a chip shop to the back and are seated in booths. You receive really authentic Chinese cuisine at very reasonable prices.

Hot & Sour Bean Curd & Vegetable Soup - £1.60, Crispy Seaweed & Nuts (V) - £2.85
*Opening Hours*
*Monday - Saturday: Noon - 3pm & 6pm - 12.30am*
*Sunday: 6.30pm - 12.30am*

## Peppers (Cafe Bar)

155 North Street
Brighton          01273 738763

**Type of Cuisine:** Various

**Breakdown:** (out of 50 dishes) **Vegetarian:** 15%; **Vegan:** 0%

Peppers is a large and classy cafe bar situated on the corner of North Street. The vegetarian dishes are imaginative and unusual. As well as the set menu there is a blackboard with daily specials.

Malaysian Fruit Medley (fruit and vegetables in a spiced Malaysian style sauce) served with Rice - £4.99, Ciabatta Melt with a Medley of Vegetables - £4.35, Vegetable Tikka Masala - £4.95, Tomato & Mozzarella Bake - £5.99

*Opening Hours*
*Monday - Saturday: 8am - 8pm      Sunday: 10am - 8pm*

## Snookie's (Restaurant)
**29 Tidy Street**
**Brighton**          01273 677712

**Type of Cuisine:** Various

**Breakdown:** (out of 40 dishes) **Vegetarian:** 40%; **Vegan:** 20%

Snookie's is named after the owner's friendly dog who wanders around the restaurant. There is a good selection of home-cooked vegetarian and vegan dishes and a homely feel.

Rich Nut Roast & Fruit Sauce (V) - £4.25, Walnut & Green Lentil Roast (V) - £4.95, Vegetable Stew - £3.90, Vegetable Curry - £3.90

*Opening Hours*
*Monday - Saturday: 10am - 10pm      Sunday: Noon - 3pm*

**Additional**
**Music:** Folk music
**Booking:** Need to book at weekends

## Surfers Paradise (Cafe)

18A Bond Street
Brighton          01273 684184
http://www.surfers-paradise.co.uk

**Type of Cuisine:** Global

**Breakdown:** (out of 30 dishes) **Vegetarian:** 10%; **Vegan:** 0%

Surfers Paradise is a net surfing, cocktail drinking kind of place with a few tempting, but exquisite, veggie treats on the menu. Ultra modern decor, trendy and surprisingly friendly. Choose from starters, light meals or main courses or just snack while you surf.

Marinated Deep Fried Tofu on a Green Bean, Mange Tout & Bean Sprout Salad, with Peanuts & Chilli Dressing - £5.95, Crispy Noodles with Stir-fried Cashew Nuts & Vegetables - £4.50, Fried Aubergine & Haloumi Cheese - £6.75

*Opening Hours*
*Every day: 10am - 7pm*

## The Bagel Bar (Take-Away)

9 Church Street
Brighton          01273 724206

**Type of Cuisine:** Bagels

**Breakdown:** (out of 80 dishes) **Vegetarian:** 50%; **Vegan:** 5%

The Bagel Bar is new to Western Road and is proving a great success. For a dinky little food bar they have a wide range of fillings and toppings for bagels and baked potatoes and the staff are very friendly.

A Bagel filled with Falafels, Homous, Avocado, Veggie Sausages, Tofu, Salad, Mozarella, Brie or Goats Cheese costs between £1.50 & £2, Jacket Potatoes - £2, Vegetable & Lentil Soup - £1.50

# bagel bar

9 CHURCH STREET & 138 WESTERN ROAD TEL: 724206/203905

## The Cheese Shop
17 Kensington Gardens
Brighton            01273 601129

**Type of Cuisine:** Cheese and deli goods

**Breakdown:** (out of 90 dishes) **Vegetarian:** 60%; **Vegan:** 30%

The Cheese Shop is a deli specialising in cheese - many of which are vegetarian. This is the place to go if you fancy an unusual lunch snack or if you want to stock up on picnic goodies.

Arbancini - Aborio rice, cheese, mushrooms & pine kernels rolled and fried - 98p, Sandwiches made to order, Pakora - 75p, Pizza Slice - £1.40, Marinated Olives and Freshly Baked Bread

*Opening Hours*

*Monday & Wednesday: 10am - 4pm*
*Tuesday, Thursday, Friday & Saturday: 9am - 5.30pm*

## The Dorset Street Bar (Cafe)

**28 North Road**
**Brighton**          01273 605423

**Type of Cuisine:** Various

**Breakdown:** (out of 50 dishes) **Vegetarian:** 20%; **Vegan:** 5%

A large stylish, trendy bar on the corner of North Road. The staff are friendly and in the summer it's a real treat to sit outside and watch the world go by. They offer slightly unusual bar food and enough vegetarian choices to make it worth a visit.

Baked Spinach & Ricotta Cannelloni - £6.85, Vegetable Provencale (Roasted Aubergine, Courgette, Peppers, Tomato and Garlic) (V) - £5.25, Fresh Basil & Garlic Pasta with Mediterranean Vegetable & Tomato Pesto - £5.25, Avocado & Tomato Croissant - £3.25

*Opening Hours*
*Monday - Saturday: 10am - 10pm*          *Sunday: 10am - 8pm*

The Dumb Waiter
Cafe

28 Sydney St., Brighton, E. Sussex BN1 4EP
(01273) 602526

# EAT WHAT THOU WILT

**Extensive vegetarian
and traditional menu:**

CLASS A CAFE

MOBILE ULTRAVIOLET CATERING UNIT

SPECIALISTS IN ORGANIC / VEGETARIAN / VEGAN FAYRE

YOU'LL LOVE US!

**ALL EVENTS
CATERED FOR -
ALLNIGHTERS
ESPECIALLY**

TELEPHONE BRIGHTON
01273-677113 / 602526

# The Dumb Waiter (Cafe)

**28 Sydney Street**
**Brighton**          **01273 602526**

**Type of Cuisine:** Breakfasts and Hot Snacks

**Breakdown:** (out of 80 dishes) **Vegetarian:** 30%; **Vegan:** 10%

The Dumb Waiter has a huge menu for such a small place. One of
the best veggie breakfasts in town is on offer and if you want to
know what's happening in Brighton, just look at the wallpaper. The
eggs are not only free-range but they come from rescued hens.

Veggie Breakfast - £3, Jacket Potatoes - from £1.45, Veggie Burgers
- £1.90, Nut Roasts (Sundays) - £4.50
*Opening Hours*
*Monday - Saturday: 9am - 5pm      Sunday: 10am - 3.30pm*

# The Grinder (Cafe)

**10 Kensington Gardens**
**Brighton**          **01273 684426**

**Type of Cuisine:** English, Italian, Oriental & Mexican

**Breakdown:** (out of 15 dishes) **Vegetarian:** 50%; **Vegan:** 15%

In one of the busiest spots in Brighton, The Grinder is great! It has
a balcony over Kensington Gardens which is popular in the
summer. Low ceilings and candles help to transform it from a
bustling day-time cafe into an evening bistro with a lovely
atmosphere. Fry-ups are the speciality, but there's also nut roast,
chilli and curries to choose from.

Pasta with Courgettes, Mushrooms, Onion, Pepper & Tomato (V) - £3.95, Stir-Fry - £3.50, Enchilada - £4.20
*Opening Hours*
*Monday - Saturday: 9am - 11pm*     *Sunday: 9am - 6pm*

# The Kensington Perk Sandwich Bar
## (Take-Away)
**15a Kensington Gardens**
**Brighton**     **01273 673776**

**Type of Cuisine:** Take-away Sandwich Bar

**Breakdown:** (out of 40 dishes) **Vegetarian:** 30%; **Vegan:** 20%

Sandwiches are made to order. You can phone and pick up your order or have it delivered.

Veg Breakfast Baguette - £2.50, Humous & Watercress (V) -£1.90, Tomato Soup - 90p, Jacket Potato with Coleslaw - £1.70, Peanut Butter & Banana Sandwich - £1.50
*Opening Hours*
*Monday - Friday: 9am - 4pm*
*Saturday: 9am - 4.30pm*     *Sunday: CLOSED*

# The George (Pub/Restaurant) ❺
**5 Trafalgar Street**
**Brighton**     **01273 681055**

**Type of Cuisine:** Vegetarian

**Breakdown:** (out of 50 dishes) **Vegetarian:** 100%; **Vegan:** 75%

The George has been given a make over and looks great. It is heaped in character, the continental-style bar being an attractive feature. There are large wooden tables, a real fire and appealing nautical thingies on the walls! The home-made veggie burgers are the best I've tasted. In fact, the food is well above your average pub standard - very appetising.

Veggie Bacon, Lettuce & Tomato Baguette, Sandwich with Mayo & Mustard - £2.50, Jacket Potato with Chilli (V) - £3, Sunday Roast (Peanut & Cashew Roast, Seasonal Vegetables, Roast Potatoes, Onion Gravy in a Yorkshire Pudding) - £4.75
*Opening Hours*
*Monday - Thursday: Noon - 8.30pm      Friday - Sunday: Noon - 7pm*
**Additional**
**Music:** Jazz and easy listening

# The Stage Door (Cafe)
**42 Sydney Street**
**Brighton**          **01273 685727**

**Type of Cuisine:** Hot Snacks

**Breakdown:** (out of 70 dishes) **Vegetarian:** 75%; **Vegan:** 10%

You can get fast food at the Stage Door Cafe and most of it is vegetarian. The veggie burgers and the chilli are vegan. There's also sandwiches, jacket potatoes and veggie breakfasts to choose from.

Veggie Breakfast (incl. drink & toast) - £3, Veggie Chilli with Chips/Jacket Potato (V) - £3, Veggie Burger - £1.60, Soup & Bread/Toast - £1.50 or 90p take-away

*Opening Hours*
*Monday - Friday: 8.45am - 4pm      Saturday: 8.45am - 5pm*

## The Thai at The Pond (Pub)

**49 Gloucester Road**
**Brighton**          01273 621400

**Type of Cuisine:** Thai

**Breakdown:** (out 23 dishes) **Vegetarian:** 50%; **Vegan:** 45%

In the evenings The Pond turns from a lunch time Purple Onion eatery into a Thai restaurant. The stir-fry dishes on the menu can be made with a choice of tofu or vegetables so many are suitable for vegetarians and vegans.

Pad Thai Noodles with Tofu - £4.95, Tempura Vegetables (Battered, Fried and Served with a Sweet Chilli Sauce) - £2.95, Praew Whaan (Tofu with Pineapple & Vegetables in a Sweet & Sour Sauce) - £4.95, Banana Fritter - £1.95
*Opening Hours*
*Monday - Saturday: 6pm - 10pm*

**Additional**
**Service:** 10% for parties of 10 or more
**Booking:** Necessary

## The Purple Onion at The Pond (Pub)

**49 Gloucester Road**
**Brighton**          01273 621400

**Type of Cuisine:** English

**Breakdown:** (out of 50 dishes) **Vegetarian:** 50%; **Vegan:** 6%
The food is cooked by vegetarian chefs. They do home-made,

wholesome veggie dishes at very reasonable prices.

Garlic & Herb Bake with Stuffed Mushrooms Topped with Brie and French Bread - £3.75, Veggie Chilli Non Carne Served on a Bed of Rice(V) - £3.25, Vegetarian Wellington - £3.75
*Opening Hours*
*Monday - Friday: Noon - 3pm*     *Saturday & Sunday: Noon - 5pm*

## The Vegetarian & Vegan Sandwich Shop
(Take-Away)
92A Trafalgar Street
Brighton          01273 623332

**Type of Cuisine:** Sandwiches

**Breakdown:** (out of 100s) **Vegetarian:** 100%; **Vegan:** 50%

Vegetarian and vegan sandwich heaven! Concoct your own amazing sarnie choosing from vegan cheese, veggie bacon, vegan coleslaw, salads, seaweed and more and stuffing it between your favourite sort of bread from focaccia to farmhouse.

Veggie BLT (Bacon, Lettuce & Tomato) (V) - £1.60, Black Olive & Tomato Pate with Salad (V) - £1.50, Vegan Cheese & Pickle - £1, Crispy Seaweed & Humous - £1.60, Greek Salad - £1.60

*Opening Hours*
*Monday - Saturday     7.30am - 5.30pm       Sunday      CLOSED*

## Wai Kika Moo Kau (Cafe)
11a Kensington Gardens
Brighton          01273 671117

**Type of Cuisine:** Global Vegetarian

**Breakdown:** (out of 20 dishes) **Vegetarian:** 100%; **Vegan:** 30%

'Totally groovy hang out joint' are the words that come to mind when I think about Wai Kika Moo Kau. An unusual name you might think, but say it over and over really slowly and it will make sense. The food is fresh and home-made and as for drinks - truly delightful. Soyaccinos (the vegan alternative to cappuccino) allow you to feel totally decadent, especially when used to wash down copious amount of vegan chocolate cake.

Main Courses on the Blackboard (e.g. Thai Curry or Stir Fry with Jasmine Rice) all at £4.50 during the day. Separate evening menu Starter & Main Course - £7.50 includes Roasted Garlic & Chestnut Soup, Mediterranean Roasted Vegetable Polenta Lasagne

*Opening Hours*
*Sunday - Tuesday: 9.30am - 6pm*
*Wednesday - Saturday: 9.30am - 10pm*

**Additional**
**Music:** 70's Soul, Jazz and Funk

## Yum-Yum Noodle Bar (Cafe)

**22-23 Sydney Street**
**Brighton**        01273 683323

**Type of Cuisine:** Maylasian, Thai, Chinese & Indonesian

**Breakdown:** (out of 30 dishes) **Vegetarian:** 33%; **Vegan:** 10%

Yum-Yums is upstairs from an oriental supermarket, both of which are charming dens of unusual and exotic foods. The selection includes mock duck which is quite a spooky taste sensation. Noodles, Rice & Spring Roll - £4.85, Singer Noodle Nasi Goren (V) - £4 - £5

*Opening Hours*
*Monday - Thursday: Noon - 6pm        Friday: Noon - 11pm*
*Saturday: Noon - 6pm        Sunday: Noon - 5.30pm*

## Zerbs (Cafe)

**21 Gardner Street**
**Brighton**        01273 685248

**Type of Cuisine:** Hot Snacks

**Breakdown:** (out of 70 dishes) **Vegetarian:** 80%; **Vegan:** 0%

A large, mainly vegetarian menu. A cafe with a difference, as well as all the usual options (jacket pots, chips, breakfasts and sandwiches), Zerbs has french bread or chips with satay sauce.

Goats Cheese & Olive Pate on French Bread - £2.25

*Opening Hours*
*Monday - Friday: 9.30am - 6pm        Saturday    9.30am - 5.30pm*

*to Vegetarian Brighton*

# THE LEVEL

## Bardsley (Cafe)

22-23-23A Baker Street
Brighton      01273 681256

**Type of Cuisine:** English Fish & Chips

**Breakdown:** (out of 50 dishes) **Vegetarian:** 20%; **Vegan:** 2%

Bardsley is a family run fish and chip shop with plenty of seating and a fun atmosphere. The chips and vegan bean burgers are well tasty.

Veggie Bean Burger - £2.60, Mushroom & Taragon Pastie - £3.25

*Opening Hours*
*Tuesday - Friday: 10.30am - 2.30pm & 4pm - 8pm*
*Saturday: 10.30am - 2.30pm*

# the george

## vegan & vegetarian

# f o o d

brighton's only vegan & vegetarian pub
quality food menu, changed regularly
booking can be made for ten or more

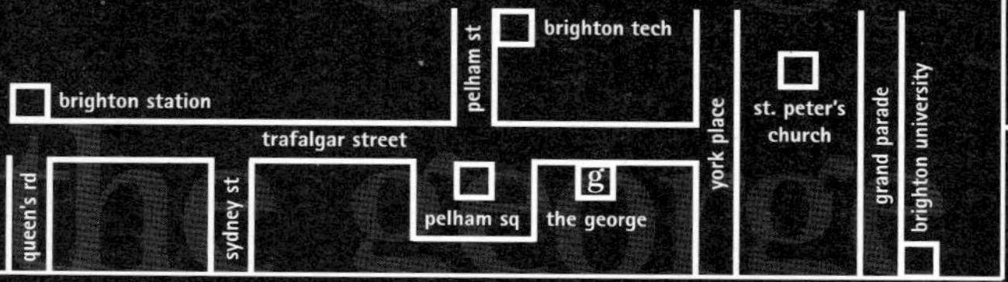

the george, 5 trafalgar st, brighton. 01273 681055

queen's rd
brighton station
sydney st
trafalgar street
pelham sq
pelham st
the george
brighton tech
york place
st. peter's church
grand parade
brighton university

food: mon-thurs 12-8.30pm
fri-sun 12-7pm
later food times in summer

heated garden (just replanted)
families welcome
relaxed atmosphere

---

the george

5/98/tva1

**25% off**

total food bill with this voucher
applies mon-thurs only

the george

5/98/tva1

**25% off**

total food bill with this voucher
applies mon-thurs only

the george

5/98/tva1

**25% off**

total food bill with this voucher
applies mon-thurs only

## Papa's (Cafe)

8 Oxford Street
Brighton          01273 699017
**Type of Cuisine:** FRIED!!

**Breakdown:** (out of 100 dishes) **Vegetarian:** 10%; **Vegan:** 0%

The great greasy spoon Papa's has got the works - burgers, omelettes, breakfasts and chips.

Veggie Breakfast - £2.65-£3.05, Egg & Chips - £1.50, Veggie Burger, Fried Onion & Chips - £2.55, Plain Omelette - £1.85, Mushroom Omelette & Chips - £2.75, Cheesey Chips - £1.60
*Opening Hours*
*Monday - Saturday: 8am - 4pm*

## Park Crescent (Pub)

39 Park Crescent Terrace
Brighton          01273 604993

**Type of Cuisine:** Various

**Breakdown:** (out of 20 dishes) **Vegetarian:** 50%; **Vegan:** 30%

The Park Crescent used to be a real locals bar - the sort of place you were scared to walk into, but now - what a transformation. Always with a friendly welcome, the staff are quick to please. It's filled with pine tables, Brighton memorabilia and although spacious, feels cosy. The food is varied, fresh and plentiful and at such good prices who can complain?

Open Baguette Veggie BLT (V) - £2.50, Veggie Shepherd's Pie (V) - £3.50, Garlic Bread - £1.95, Humous with Pitta Bread & Crudites (V) - £2.50, Veggie Breakfast - £3.50, Vegetable Curry (V)- £3.95, Veggie Chilli (V)- £3.30

*Opening Hours*
*Monday - Saturday: 5.30pm - 8pm    Sunday: 12.30pm - 3.30pm*

**Additional**
**Music:** Funky soul, acid jazz & indie
**Organic:** Lots of organic vegetables and bread are used

# Shada Thai Cuisine (Restaurant)

4 Lewes Road
Brighton          01273 677608

**Breakdown:** (out of 69 dishes) **Vegetarian:** 50%; **Vegan:** 5%

Shada offer an extensive and truly delicious range of sauces - sweet and sour, black bean, yellow curry and many more - as basic dishes which you can choose to have with tofu and vegetables. Although the Lewes Road location is quite grim, inside this restaurant it is rich and colourful. Let your karma be purified while you wallow in the presence of Buddha images and soft candle light.

Yellow Curry with Tofu - £4.75, Shada Pad Roum with Spicy Mixed Vegetables Wok Fried in Spicy Sauce - £4.95

*Opening Hours*
*Monday - Saturday: 6.45pm - 10.30pm    Sunday: 7pm - 10.30pm*

**Additional**
**Music:** Modern ambient
**Booking:** Necessary at the weekends

### The Sir Charles Napier (Pub)

50 Southover Street
Brighton      01273 601413

**Type of Cuisine:** Traditional pub food

**Breakdown:** (out of 30+ dishes) **Vegetarian:** 45%; **Vegan:** 0%

This is a pub with a beer garden ideal for summer lunches and snacks. The food is freshly prepared and very reasonably priced. But it's a packet of crisps and a coke for the vegans!

Veggie Bake and Special Roll - Stilton, Mango Chutney, Salad & Mayo on French Bread - £2, Cauliflower Cheese - £2.50, Macaroni Cheese - £2.30, Beau Broccoli - £3, Veggie Curry - £2.75
*Opening Hours*
*Every day: Noon - 2pm*

**Additional**
**Music:** Various    **Booking:** Large groups need to book
**Organic:** Suppliers use mainly organic produce

## THE LANES

### Ask (Restaurant)

Duke Street
Brighton      01273 710030

**Type of Cuisine:** Italian

**Breakdown:** (out of 40 dishes) **Vegetarian:** 20%; **Vegan:** 10%

Ask is a new restaurant to Brighton and it looks it. The decor is very striking, ultra modern and spacious - covering five floors! They serve mainly pasta, pizzas and salads; classic Italian with a gourmet touch. Top quality. The toilets are fantastic - well worth a visit too!

Pizza Vegetariana - £5.40, Spaghetti al Pomodoro (V) £4.90, Mushrooms al Forno (Baked Mushrooms Stuffed with Parmesan, Garlic & Breadcrumbs) - £3.40, Penne con Pomodori Secchi (Sun-dried Tomatoes, Artichokes, Basil, Chillies and Olive Oil) - £5.75

*Opening Hours*
*Every day: Noon - Midnight*

**Additional**
**Service:** 10% optional charge on parties of 7 or more
**Booking:** Necessary at weekends


# Barkers (Cafe)

**17/18 Dukes Lane**
**Brighton**          01273 325945

**Type of Cuisine:** Various

**Breakdown:** (out of 80 dishes) **Vegetarian:** 10%; **Vegan:** 2%

Barkers has the feel of a franchise. The vegetarian options are there, but lack imagination.

Vegetarian Cannelloni - £4.95, Jacket Potato with Baked Beans - £3.50, Garlic Bread - £1.25, Omelettes - £4, Vegetarian Pizza - £5.50

*Opening Hours*
*Monday - Thursday: 9am - 11pm*
*Friday: 9am - 11pm      Saturday: 9am - 6pm*

## Barry at The Tureen (Pub)
**31 Upper North Street**
**Brighton**          **01273 328939**

**Type of Cuisine:** Continental

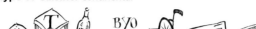

**Breakdown:** (out of 15 dishes) **Vegetarian:** 15%; **Vegan:** 0%

Barry loves his lambs' kidneys and calves liver, but if that doesn't put you off going through the door, then there is a creative veggie option in there for you. The menu changes regularly, so it might be worth a phone call to check what's on offer.

Individual Caramelised Red Onion & Sun-dried Tomato Tart followed by a Pancake with asparagus, tomato, mushrooms and vegetarian cheddar (- £16 for two courses) and if you can face it a Baked Apple & Almond Sponge & Custard - £18 (for three courses)
*Opening Hours*
*Tuesday - Saturday: from 7pm*

## Barton's (Cafe)
**7-8 Prince Albert Street**
**Brighton**          **01273 729474**

**Type of Cuisine:** Italian & English

**Breakdown:** (out of 110 dishes) **Vegetarian:** 20%; **Vegan:** 1%

Barton's is a large restaurant - with a large bar! - but feels intimate. It's busy with typical Italian feel and a good vegetarian selection. The vegetarian salad is amazing (and it's vegan) so tuck into the tasty, healthy platter of delight.

Vegetarian Salad (humous, avocado, stuffed vine leaves & artichoke) (V) -£6.95, Garlic Bread - £1.55, Baked Onion Stuffed with Ricotta & Spinach - £3.95, Spinach, Egg & Mushroom Pizza - £5.50, Apple Crumble - £3.25

*Opening Hours*
*Every day: 11.30am - 11pm*
**Additional**
**Service:** 10% added to bill
**Booking:** No need

# Bella Pasta (Restaurant)

**24 Market Street**
**Brighton**        01273 777607

**Type of Cuisine:** Italian Pasta & Pizza

**Breakdown:** (out fo 50 dishes) **Vegetarian:** 50%; **Vegan:** 0%

Bella Pasta is a friendly and pleasant chain of Italian restaurants dotted around the country. The food is good and reasonably priced and they have plenty of vegetarian options. They have no vegan dishes at the moment but they are looking into it so watch this space.

Gnocchi Al Quattro Formaggi (Traditional Potato Pasta Baked in an Italian Four Cheese & Herb Sauce) - £3.95, Al Pesto Genovese (Traditional Pesto made with Basil, Pine Kernels, Garlic, Olive Oil and Parmesan Cheese) - £5.45

*Opening Times*
*Sunday - Thursday: 11am-11pm        Friday & Saturday: 11am-Midnight*

**Additional**
**Service:** 10% for parties of 8 or more
**Booking:** Necessary at weekends

## Bombay Aloo (Restaurant) ❶

Ship Street
Brighton          01273 773804

**Type of Cuisine:** Vegetarian Indian Buffet

**Breakdown:** (out of 15 dishes) **Vegetarian:** 100%; **Vegan:** 60%

Bombay Aloo has a bistro feel and offers a buffet of 15 tasty vegetarian dishes many of which are vegan - so you can pick and choose. There are plenty of pickles and sauces as well as naan to enhance the flavours of India. Help yourself again and again until you're fit to burst. This popular restaurant is excellent value.

Vegetarian Indian Buffet - £4.50

*Opening times*
*Everyday: Noon - Midnight*

## Cactus Canteen (Restaurant)

5 Brighton Square
Brighton          01273 725700

**Type of Cuisine:** Mexican

**Breakdown:** (out of 60-70 dishes) **Vegetarian:** 15%; **Vegan:** 0%

The Cactus Canteen is big - really big! It's got a funky, friendly feel and cactus paintings give it that authentic touch. The food is freshly prepared on the premises and there are plenty of veggie options.

Cajun Mushrooms - £3.95, Yucatan Burritos - £8.95, Jumping Bean Salad - £6.95, Santa Fe Skins with Vegetable Chilli - £3.50, Tacos Mexicano - £7.95, Canteen Burgers, Avocado, Beef Tomato & Chips or a Jacket - £7.95, Hot Fudge Brownies - £3.75

*Opening Hours*
*Every day: 11.30am - 11pm*

**Additional**
**Booking:** Necessary at weekends

## Cafe Rouge (Cafe)

**24 Prince Albert Street**
**Brighton**                   **01273 774422**

**Type of Cuisine:** French

**Breakdown:** (out of 30+ dishes) **Vegetarian:** 10%; **Vegan:** 0%

Cafe Rouge is a nice restaurant in a pretty part of town. There are enough vegetarian dishes to make you feel welcome, but they are way too cheesy for vegans.

Bourse a la Grecque (Spinach, Feta Cheese and Pine Kernels in Filo Pastry) - £6.50, Salade aux Champignons (Wild Mushrooms, Penne & Pine Kernels with Coriander & Sesame Dressing) - £3.50, Deep-Fried Camembert with Red Currant Sauce - £3.75
*Opening Hours*
*Monday - Saturday: 10am - 11pm      Sunday: 10am - 10.30pm*

**Additional**
**Booking:** Necessary at weekends

## Caffe Uno (Restaurant)

27 North Street
Brighton       01273 329091

**Type of Cuisine:** Italian

**Breakdown:** (out of 70 dishes) **Vegetarian:** 20%; **Vegan:** 0%

A busy modern continental-style restaurant which has a good selection of dishes. Make sure you look at the daily specials board as they are often veggie. The pizzas are freshly made and sauces all home made.

Calzone Al Formaggi (Folded Pizza with Mozzarella, Ricotta Cheese, Gorgonzola, fresh tomatoes & spinach) - £6.45, Insalata Di Mozzarella (Thick Slices of Mozzarella with Roasted Vegetables) - £3.75, Tiramisu - £3.25

*Opening Hours*
*Monday - Friday: 10am - 11pm*
*Saturday: 10am - Midnight*     *Sunday: Noon - 10.30pm*

## Cybar   (Cafe/Bar)

9-12 Middle Street
Brighton       01273 384280
www.cybar.co.uk

**Type of Cuisine:** Global

**Breakdown:** (out of 20 dishes) **Vegetarian:** 50%; **Vegan:** 10%

The Cybar is the perfect pre-club bar or lunch out place. The decor

# CAFFÉ UNO

## *Welcome to Brighton's newest Italian Bar, Restaurant & Caffé*

* Pizza Freshly made to order
* Homemade sauces & freshly prepared pasta
* Daily Specials
* Tea, coffee, cakes & snacks served all day
* Fully licensed
* Bar open all day for drinks - no need to eat - just relax in our bar
* Traditional & continental breakfast served 9am-12noon
* A Wide range of freshly prepared sandwiches, baguettes & snacks
* Open 7 days a week

## 27 NORTH ST BRIGHTON TEL: 01273 329091

is very modern yellows, purple and turquoise with chic furniture and lighting. The coffee is tasty and there's always a veggie option on the menu which changes weekly. The chef is willing to cater for vegans and will alter dishes to suit your needs. Bar snacks are available all day such as vegetarian sushi, marinated mushrooms and various pasties. You can also surf the net - £2.50 per half hour.

Tofu Rice Paper Parcels with Ginger Rice & Side Salad - £5.95, Greek Salad - £2.50, Carrot, Zucchini & Corriander Soup - £2.50, Avocado, Mozarella & Tomato Open Doorstep Sandwich - £3.95, Rich Dark Chocolate Marquis - £1.95
*Opening Hours*
*Every day: Noon - 3pm & 7pm - 10pm*

### Additional
**Music:** Live bands, comedy, cabaret and DJs at weekends.

## Esprit (Take-Away)
**41 Market Street**
**Brighton          01273 748801**

**Type of Cuisine:** Sandwiches and cakes

**Breakdown:** (out of 60 dishes) **Vegetarian:** 10%; **Vegan:** 5%

Classy, clean and trendy, Esprit caters for the modern muncher. Basically, choose your ideal filling combination and have the sandwich of your dreams.

Stilton & Salad Roll - £1.50 or Humous & Salad Roll (V) - £1.25, Feta Cheese Salad Roll - £1.50, Egg Mayo & Cress Baguette - £1.75, Carrot Cake - 95p, Shortbread - 60p
*Opening Hours*
*Every day: 7am - 6pm*

# Food For Friends (Restaurant)  ❸

17a-18 Prince Albert Street
The Lanes
Brighton          01273 202310

**Type of Cuisine:** Global Vegetarian

**Breakdown:** (out of 10 dishes) **Vegetarian:** 100%; **Vegan:** 20%

As well as cooking all their food fresh every day (menus change daily), Food for Friends is a delightful vegetarian and vegan haven for visitors to the town. Basically you must go, even if it's just for a coffee and a vegan chocolate cake! Situated in The Lanes, this is a perfect stop off from a shopping spree. Let the mellow hums of Van Morrison and Everything But The Girl wash your credit card bill blues away and watch the world go by. In the evening, it transforms from a busy cafe feel to a romantic restaurant with pine tables, candles and fresh flowers. Oh! the food is totally yummy, plentiful and cheap too!

Aubergine & Broccoli Roly-poly with Roasted Pepper Sauce (V) - £4.95, Moussaka Aphrodite - £3.20, Broccoli & Mange-tout Quiche - £1.95, Green Split Pea & Mint Soup (V) - £1.45,  Banoffi Pie - £1.35

**Additional**
**Music:** Everything But The Girl, Van Morrison, Classical, Portishead

*Opening Hours*
*Monday - Saturday: 8am - 10pm*
*Sunday: 9.15am - 10pm*

# Food for friends

*17a-18 Prince Albert Street, The Lanes, Brighton BN1 1HF Tel: 01273 202310*
*Licensed Vegetarian & Vegan Restaurant*
*open from 8am-10pm everyday for Breakfast, Lunch, Afternoon Tea & Dinner*
*-Organic Wines, Soya Alternatives & Allergy Aware-*
*Global Food at Pastoral Prices*
*Reservations on 01273 202310*

## Greens (Cafe Bar)
**62 West Street**
**Brighton**　　　**01273 778579**

**Type of Cuisine:** English, Italian & French

**Breakdown:** (out of 17 dishes) **Vegetarian:** 50%; **Vegan:** 0%

Greens is a new bar and cafe with breakfasts, light bites and a couple of veggie main courses on the menu.

Deep Fried Vegetables £2.50, Tortellini Ricotta - £4.75, Corn on the Cob - £2.50, Garlic Mushrooms - £3.75, Danish Pastry - 95p
*Opening Hours*
*Every day: Noon - 6pm*

## Jacco's (Restaurant)

14 East Street
Brighton          01273 206554

**Type of Cuisine:** Italian

**Breakdown:** (out of 50 dishes) **Vegetarian:** 10%; **Vegan:** 0%

Large, atmospheric restaurant with friendly staff and a few good veggie choices.

Tagliatelle Vegetarian (courgettes, sweetcorn & spinach in a cream sauce) - £5.45, Garlic Mushrooms - £3.45, Zucchini Pizza - £5.45, Vegetarian Cannelloni or Spaghetti - £5.25, Deep Fried Onion Rings - £1.10, Pancakes with Ice Cream - £3.45
*Opening Hours*
*Every day: Noon - 11pm*

**Additional**
**Service:** 10% service charge will be added to the bill

## Moon's (Cafe & Brasserie)

42 Meeting House Lane
Brighton          01273 323824
moons@mistral.co.uk

**Type of Cuisine:** English/European

**Breakdown: Vegetarian:** 60%; **Vegan:** 5%

Fresh daily specials always include a vegetarian dish. Moon's is a nice place to hang out and snack or feast 'til your bursting.

Roasted Red Peppers (stuffed with sun-dried tomatoes, shallots, black olives and garlic) - £6.55, Mushroom Strudel - £6.75, Vegetarian Breakfast - £4.25, Soup & Salad - £3.75, Baked Avocado with Stilton - £3.50, Garlic Mushrooms - £3.45

*Opening Hours*
*Sunday - Thursday: 8am - 6pm*
*Friday & Saturday: 8am - 10pm*

**Additional**
**Music:** Tapes ranging from the 40's to the 80's
**Service:** 10% service on parties of 5 or more
**Booking:** Necessary on Friday and Saturday evenings

## Old Orleans (Restaurant)

**1-3 Prince Albert Street**
**Brighton**          **01273 747000**

**Type of Cuisine:** American

**Breakdown:** (out of 100 dishes) **Vegetarian:** 20%; **Vegan:** 0%

Old Orleans invites you to enjoy their Southern hospitality, a veggie burger and a cocktail to wash it down - hic!

Veggie Special (wholesome bean-burgers, coated in golden breadcrumbs & topped with melted cheeses) - £6.95, Potato & Cheese Chowder - £3.35, Onion Rings - £1.50, Fried Mozzarella with a Sliced Apple & Mustard Dip - £3.10

*Opening Hours*
*Every day: 11am - 11pm*

## Piccolo (Restaurant)

56 Ship Street
Brighton          01273 380380

**Type of Cuisine:** Italian

**Breakdown:** (out of 40 dishes) **Vegetarian:** 50%; **Vegan:** 10%

The food is prepared to order and the chef promises to be flexible.
So just let them know your requirements and they will feed you.
Good quality Italian food is the order of the day and there's a few
tasty vegan treats too!

Margarita Pizza - £3.30, Ravioli Bosciola - £4.90,
Spaghetti Napoletana (V) - £4.20
*Opening Hours*
*Every day: Noon - Midnight*
**Additional**
**Music:** Mediterranean and Soul Music
**Service:** 10% service charge for parties of 6 or over

## Pizza Express (Restaurant)

22 Prince Albert Street
The Lanes
Brighton          01273 323205

**Type of Cuisine:** Italian Pizza

**Breakdown:** (out of 20 dishes) **Vegetarian:** 40%; **Vegan:** 15%

Popular franchise with chic black and white decor. The pizzas are delicious. If you're vegan don't be put off - just say no to the cheese.

Florentina Pizza £4.90, Venziana (ask for no cheese)(V) - £4.20
*Opening Hours*
*Every day: 11.30am - 12pm*

**Additional:**
**Music:** Jazz, soul etc.


# Platters (Cafe)
**26 Dukes Lane**
**Brighton          01273 749377**

**Type of Cuisine:** Sandwiches, Salads and Soups

**Breakdown:** (out of 60 dishes) **Vegetarian:** 40%; **Vegan:** 2%

Friendly helpful staff is what you'll find at Platters. All the healthy salad boxes are vegetarian and there's plenty of sandwich options to choose from. Often the soup is vegan, but if not, there's onion bhajis or samosas to choose from.

Salad Box - £1.50, Garlic & Mushroom Pasty £1.80, Vegetable Samosa (V) - £1.50, Vegetarian Sausage Sandwich - £1.60, Avocado Salad Sandwich - £1.30

*Opening Hours*
*Monday - Saturday: 9am - 5pm*

## Soul Jazz on Sea (Cafe)

62 Middle Street
Brighton          01273 776526

**Type of Cuisine:** Sandwiches and Hot Snacks

**Breakdown:** (out of 70 dishes) **Vegetarian:** 70%; **Vegan:** 20%

The Soul Jazz on Sea is surprisingly... a cafe playing soul and jazz by
the sea! Offering the most unusual breakfast I have ever come
across in Brighton and playing some rare grooves makes snacking
here a real treat. It's a place to chill out and read a mag or two
amongst brightly coloured, funky surroundings.

Breakfast Huevos Ranchos (tortilla, poached egg, guacamole,
cheese & salad with fried potatoes) - £3.50, Humous, Carrot & Salad
Baguette (V) - £3.50
*Opening Hours*
*Tuesday - Sunday: Noon - 6pm*

## Sun Bo Seng (Restaurant)

70 East Street
Brighton          01273 323108

**Type of Cuisine:** Chinese

**Breakdown:** (out of 100 dishes) **Vegetarian:** 20%; **Vegan:** 2%

This sophisticated restaurant serves quality authentic Chinese food
in an authentic Chinese setting. There is a vegetarian section in the
menu with plenty of delectable dishes to choose from.

Meal for two including - Seaweed, Spring Rolls, Crispy Aubergines, French Beans in Black-Bean Sauce & Sweet & Spicy Beancurd - £12 per person, Beancurd with Peanuts and Vegetables in a Yellow Bean Sauce (V) - £3.20

*Opening Hours*
*Monday - Friday: Noon - 2pm & 5.30pm - 11pm*
*Saturday & Sunday: Noon - 11pm*
**Additional:**
**Booking:** Necessary at weekends

## Terre A Terre (Restaurant)
71 East Street
Brighton          01273 729051

**Type of Cuisine:** Global Vegetarian

**Breakdown:** (out of 30 dishes) **Vegetarian:** 100%; **Vegan:** 50%

Terre a Terre has recently moved to more spacious premises which is a reflection of their success and popularity. Serving excellent vegetarian and vegan cuisine for many years now, they really know what they're doing and they do it well. If you're in Brighton visit this distinctive and contemporary restaurant. The prices are reasonable and the food is presented beautifully and tastes exquisite. Go on treat your taste-buds!

Sushi (V) (Roasted nori rice rolls filled with pickled ginger and sweet pepper served with Yokohama Sampan along with dipping sauce and wasabi) - £4.50, Thai Green Curry (V) - £7.75, Soup & Warmed Bread (V) - £2.90
*Opening Hours*
*Tuesday - Sunday: Noon - 10.30pm     Monday: 6pm - 10.30pm*
**Additional**
**Music:** Various mellow tunes
**Service:** No charge
**Booking:** Necessary - especially at the weekend

## Thai Spice Market (Restaurant)

**13 Boyces Street**
**Brighton**      01273 325195

**Type of Cuisine:** Thai

**Breakdown:** (out of 70 dishes) **Vegetarian:** 30%; **Vegan:** 20%

This is Thai home cooking at its best. A cosy, characterful intimate restaurant which has a wide selection of vegetarian and vegan dishes. I recommend the set menu for two.

Set menu for two includes Hot & Sour Chopped Mushrooms and Crispy Noodles Flavoured with Tamarind, followed by Beancurd Curry, Mushrooms and Cashew Nuts with Chilli, Noodles and Fragrant Rice (£12.50 each).

*Opening Hours*
*Monday - Saturday: 6pm - 11pm*
**Additional**
**Service:** 10% service charge

## The Coffee Company Ltd (Cafe)

**16 Prince Albert Street**
**Brighton**          01273 220222

**Type of Cuisine:** Premium Coffee and pastries

**Breakdown:** (out of 10 dishes) **Vegetarian:** 100%; **Vegan:** 0%

If you need to get a caffeine hit, then this is the place. The Coffee Company has a huge selection of premium coffee and a bar for you to sit and kick back. The Coffee Company is situated in The Lanes so it's handy for shoppers who want a treat.

Coffee, Cakes & Pastries at various prices.
*Opening Hours*
*Monday - Friday: 8am - 6pm*
*Saturday: 8am - 10pm*          *Sunday: 9am - 6pm*

## The Druid's Head (pub)

**9 Brighton Place**
**Brighton**          01273 325490

**Type of Cuisine:** Lunch Time Bar Food

**Breakdown:** (out of 20 dishes) **Vegetarian:** 25%; **Vegan:** 0%

The Druids Head is very dark inside which adds to the atmosphere of the place, but I don't think I'd like to be in there on a glorious hot sunny day. The bar food is up on blackboards and there is a separate board for vegetarian specials. But, what's on offer is not so special - lasagne, vegetable kiev or cheese and broccoli bake and nothing for vegans.

Three Cheese & Broccoli Bake, Vegetarian Lasagne or Vegetable Kiev all with Fries or Salad and followed by Apple Pie and Tea or Coffee for £4.50
*Opening Hours*
*Every day: 12pm - 5pm*
**Additional:**
**Music:** Rock duke box

# The Meeting House (Cafe)

**19 Meeting House Lane**
**Brighton**          **01273 324817**

**Type of Cuisine:** European/English Hot Snacks

**Breakdown:** (out of 70 dishes) **Vegetarian:** 20%; **Vegan:** 0%

The usual cafe vegetarian options on offer here - lasagne, quiche, veggie burger or veggie breakfast and nothing for vegans. However it is a nice, spacious, clean cafe and the staff are very helpful.

Quiche & Salad with Chips/Jacket Potato - £3.95, Vegetarian Lasagne - £4.95, Veggie Breakfast - £3.95, Veggie Burger with Chips or Jacket Potato or Salad - £3.95

*Opening Hours*
*Monday - Saturday: 9am - 5pm    Sunday: 10am - 5pm*

## The Strand (Restaurant)

**6 Little East Street**
**Brighton**          **01273 747096**

**Type of Cuisine:** Global

**Breakdown:** (out of 35 dishes) **Vegetarian:** 30%; **Vegan:** 5%

The Strand is relatively new to Brighton and feels cosy and special. They have quality food so if you fancy something a bit different this is the place. Choose from the menu or the three course set vegetarian menu for £9.95. The vegan choice is limited, but as the food is all freshly prepared, the staff are willing to adapt a dish to suit your needs.

Apple & Potato Rosties with Walnut & Stilton Sauce - £8.95, Roasted Aubergines with Fresh Basil & Cous Cous (V) - £7.95, Deep Fried Brie - £3.50, Parsnip Crisps with a Creme Fraiche Dip - £2.95.

*Opening Hours*
*Every day: Noon - 10pm*
**Additional**
**Service:** Not included
**Booking:** Necessary at weekends

## The Waffle House (Cafe/Restaurant)

**36 Ship Street**
**Brighton**          **01273 747808**

**Type of Cuisine:** Waffles - Savoury & Sweet

**Breakdown:** (out of 50 dishes) **Vegetarian:** 70%; **Vegan:** 20%

The Waffle House is near to the central shopping area of Brighton and is a pleasant break from the hustle and bustle of town. Quality pine furniture, tasteful but simple decor and mellow tunes make you want to melt. The staff at the Waffle House are always very friendly and willing to accommodate various diets. The Waffle House is also the cafe location featured on the Viva! video - Food For Life.

Ratatouille With Rice (V) or Waffle - £3.75, Nut Pate with Salad or a Waffle - £4.95, Garlic Mushrooms with a Waffle - £3.75
*Opening Hours*
*Monday - Saturday: 9.30am - 11pm*        *Sunday: 10.30am - 10pm*
**Additional**
**Music:** Classical & Light Jazz
**Service:** Not included
**Booking:** Necessary on Saturday night

## Victor's (Restaurant)
**11 Little East Street**
**Brighton**        **01273 774545**

**Type of Cuisine:** Traditional French Cuisine

**Breakdown: Vegetarian:** 20%; **Vegan:** 5%

Tasty vegetarian French Cuisine is available at Victor's and there's a few imaginative dishes to choose from, even for vegans which is more than I found in Paris a couple of years ago!

Platter with a Selection of Vegetables with Red Pepper Coulis -

TREAT YOURSELF
to
THE WAFFLE HOUSE
Experience

Delicious food at affordable prices
some fresh organic ingredients
Bring this advertisement to enjoy 10% off a meal
value of £5 per person any number of people

£10.85, Papillote of Vegetable with Curry (V) - £9.75
*Opening Hours*
*Every day: Noon - 3pm & 7pm - 10.30pm*
**Additional**
**Booking:** Necessary

### Alice's (Cafe)
**113 St George's Road**
**Kemptown**
**Brighton**          01273 675351

**Type of Cuisine:** Coffee Shop & Take-Away

**Breakdown:** (out of 50 dishes) **Vegetarian:** 30%; **Vegan:** 0%
This Kemptown cafe is one of the most popular in the area probably as it has lots of choices on the menu and because the staff are friendly. The veggie selection is quite basic - jacket potatoes, macaroni cheese and such like, but good snacks.

Macaroni Cheese, Salad & Chips - £3.75, Stilton & Chestnut Pate Baguette - £2.30, Veggie Breakfast - £3.50, Welsh Rarebit - £2, Mushroom Omelette £2.50, Jacket Potato with Home-made Coleslaw - £2.35
*Opening Hours*
*Monday - Friday: 9.30am - 4pm     Saturday & Sunday: 9.30am - 3pm*

# Biederhoff's (Take-Away)

**176 Edward Street**
**Kemptown**
**Brighton**          **01273 570392**

**Type of Cuisine:** Sandwiches and Hot Snacks

**Breakdown:** (out of 100 dishes) **Vegetarian:** 40%; **Vegan:** 0%

Biederhoffs's claim to provide the best sandwiches in town. All the sandwiches are made to order with generous Deli-style fillings.

Veggie Italiano Toasted Sandwich - £3.20, Mixed Salad Sandwich - £1, French Brie & Red & Green Pepper Sandwich - £1.90, Cream Cheese & Pineapple Sandwich - £1.60
*Opening Hours*
*Monday - Friday: 9am - 2pm*

# Cafe Bohemia (Cafe)

**57 St James's Street**
**Kemptown**
**Brighton**          **01273 609832**

**Type of Cuisine:** Breakfasts & Hot Snacks

**Breakdown:** (out of 30 dishes) **Vegetarian:** 10%; **Vegan:** 0%

Cafe Bohemia is the place for the hungry veggie - check out the mega veggie breakfast if you want to fuel up.

Mega Veggie Breakfast - £4.95, Regular Veggie Breakfast - £2.60, Chips & Beans (V) - £1.30, Veggie Burger & Chips - £2.75, Jacket Potatoes - from £1.20
*Opening Hours*
*Every day: 8am - 6pm*

## Cruickshank's Kemptown Deli

**108 St George's Road**
**Kemptown**
**Brighton**          01273 603411

**Type of Cuisine:** Deli Cheeses, bread, olives, biscuits, juices & pasties

**Breakdown:** (out of 100's of dishes) **Vegetarian:** 60%; **Vegan:** 2%

The Kemp Town Deli has an amazing range of cheeses, pasties, sandwiches, breads, jams and biscuits. They also sell fresh home-made pesto and organic juices such as Apple and Cinnamon Juice.

Mature Farmhouse Cheddar Cheese & Crisp Apple Sandwich - £1.60
Vegetable Pakora - 75p, Apple & Cinnamon Juice - £2.25, Spinach & Cream Cheese Pasty - 90p
*Opening Hours*
*Monday - Saturday: 9am - 6pm*

## Happy Dragon (Restaurant)

**111 St George's Road**
**Kemptown**
**Brighton**

**Type of Cuisine:** Chinese

**Breakdown:** (out of 200 dishes) **Vegetarian:** 10%; **Vegan:** 0%

Tasty Chinese cuisine to tempt your taste buds at this place. There's not much in the way of vegetarian options but what there is will put a smile on your face and an extra few pounds on your waist line.

Crispy Wun Tun with Cashews £2.95 followed by Chinese Leaves with Garlic/Blackbean Sauce - £3.50
*Opening Hours      Monday - Saturday: 12pm - 2pm & 5pm - 11pm*

## Jesters (Restaurant)
**87 St James's Street, Kemptown**
**Brighton          01273 624233**

**Type of Cuisine:** Mediterranean

**Breakdown:** (out of 60 dishes) **Vegetarian:** 15%; **Vegan:** 0%

Jester's is a gay, cosy and friendly restaurant in Kemp Town. They do a good selection of veggie dishes.

Asparagus in Creamy Parmesan and Wine Sauce - £6.95, Black Olive & Kidney Bean Pate with Warm Toast - £3.25, Five Bean Chilli - £7.50, Fried Brie Wedges & Cranberry Couli - £3.95
*Opening Hours*
*Every day:  5.30pm - 10.30pm*

## Le Cafe De Paris (Pub)

**40 St James's Street, Kemptown**
**Brighton**        01273 603740

**Type of Cuisine:** Various pub food

**Breakdown:** (out of 100 dishes) **Vegetarian:** 10%; **Vegan:** 0%

Amazing tasty vegetarian bargain alert! Five courses for £5.95. Too good to be true - see for yourself!
Garlic Bread, Soup, Nutty Salad, Orange & Ginger Nut Roast & Desert - £5.95, Deep Fried Brie in Filo - £5.25, Vegetable Pancake - £4.50
*Opening Times*
*Monday-Friday: 5.30pm - 10.30pm    Saturday & Sunday: 11.30am - 11.45pm*

## Market Diner (Cafe)

**9 Circus Street,**
**Brighton**        01273 725249

**Type of Cuisine:** Fast Food

**Breakdown:** (out of 30 dishes) **Vegetarian:** 20%; **Vegan:** 0%

This is the place to go if you happen to be either a market trader or an insomniac. Yes, it's open all night so beat those midnight munchies, head for the Market Diner and treat yourself to an all night breakfast. They can do a vegan version if you ask them nicely.

Vegi-Buster (just about everything you can think of in a greasy spoon) - £3.40, Beans on Toast (V), Egg & Chips, Mushrooms on Toast, Veggie Burgers etc.

## Muang Thai (Restaurant)

**77 St James's Street**
**Brighton**        **01273 605223**

**Type of Cuisine:** Thai

**Breakdown:** (out of 100 dishes) **Vegetarian:** 10%; **Vegan:** 0%

The vegetarian set menu has some tasty treats. The decor is sparce and classy, and the food is rich and tasty.

Vegetarian Set Menu - Sa-Tay Hed (mushrooms with peanut sauce), Mim Thai Spring Rolls, Fried Mung Bean Noodles, Fried Bean Curd, Red Curry & Rice with a Desert to complete - £12.95

*Opening Hours*
*Every day: 12.30pm - 3pm & 6.30pm - 12am*

## Naff Caff (Cafe)

**40-42 Upper St James's Street**
**Kemptown**
**Brighton**        **01273 626060**

**Type of Cuisine:** All-day Breakfasts & Sandwiches

**Breakdown:** (out of 50 dishes) **Vegetarian:** 40%; **Vegan:** 20%

The front of the Naff Caff has large windows so the sunlight streams in and makes the place feel bright and spacious. The green and cream decor is clean and fresh. Veggies and vegans are well catered for with a separate blackboard menu full of options.

Veggie Breakfast (egg, 2 sausages, beans, tomatoes, fried potatoes, mushrooms, tea/coffee & toast/bread & butter) - £4.35, 2 Veggie Sausages, Mash, Beans & Onion Gravy (V) - £3.25, Veggie Bubble & Squeak - £3.25

*Opening Hours*
*Monday - Saturday: 8am-4pm*                    *Sunday: 9am-4pm*

## Samson's (Restaurant)

**25 St George's Road**
**Kemptown**
**Brighton**

**Type of Cuisine:** Various

**Breakdown:** (out of 30 dishes) **Vegetarian:** 20%; **Vegan:** 0%

The decor in Samson's is clean, fresh dark green with plenty of antique pine. The veggie options are unimaginative but at least they exist.

Deep Fried Vegetables in Batter with Sweet & Sour Dip - £2.95, Lasagne - £4.95, Stuffed Mushrooms - £2.95, Jacket Potato loaded with Cheese, Sour Cream, Chives and Veggie Bacon Bits with Salad - £3.25

*Opening Hours*
*Every day: 6pm - 10.30*

### The Barley Mow (Pub)

92 St George's Street
Kemptown
Brighton

**Type of Cuisine:** Pub Food

**Breakdown:** (out or 40 dishes) **Vegetarian:** 40%; **Vegan:** 0%

The Barley Mow Pub offers a few good choices for vegetarians at reasonable prices. No children.

Deep Fried Camembert Cheese with Red Currant Sauce - £2.50, Mushroom Stroganoff - £3, Vegetable Chilli - £3, Vegetable Curry - £3, Pasta with Tomato Sauce - £3, Leek & Potato Soup - £1.75
*Opening Hours*
*Every day (for food): Noon - 2pm*

### The Burlington (Pub)

8 St George's Road
Kemptown
Brighton          01273 683334

**Type of Cuisine:** Everything

**Breakdown:** (out of 20/30 dishes) **Vegetarian:** 100%; **Vegan:** 75%

Dan and Chris, the Burly chefs have been vegetarians for many years, so they know what they're doing and they do it well. The pub is spacious, contemporary with a really welcoming feel about it. The food is home-made, even down to the dressings, dips and pates. The prices are very reasonable and there's a wide range of dishes to choose from - for vegans too.

Choose from a Veggie BLT (V), Hempseed Burger (V), Soup of the day (V) or a Traditional Greek Salad. Sunday Lunch (a generous portion of moist, traditional nut roast, served with cranberry stuffing, Yorkshire pudding, roast potatoes, 3 seasonal vegetables in a rich mustard & onion gravy) - £4.50 and to finish an Orange Sorbet with Maple Syrup - £1.95

*Opening Hours*
*Monday - Friday: 11am - 9.30pm      Saturday & Sunday: 11am - 6.30pm*

---

### DAN & CHRIS WELCOME YOU TO

# The Burlington Pub

8 St George's Road, Kemptown.
Tel: 01273 683334

## THE LARGEST 100% VEGGIE & VEGAN MENU IN BRIGHTON
(Including Gluten Free & Wheat Free Options)

Lunches, All Day Breakfasts, Dinners, Sandwiches, Snacks, Specials, Lightbites, Deserts, Bookings, Take-away &

### SPECIAL SUNDAY ROAST

**open everyday, all day & early evenings**

---

### The Plaice to Meat (Cafe)

97 St James's Street
Kemptown
Brighton          01273 693498

**Type of Cuisine:** Hot Snacks

**Breakdown:** (out of 100 dishes) **Vegetarian:** 20%; **Vegan:** 5%

It was a real surprise meeting the manager of the Plaice to Meat and discovering he is really into vegetarian food - so much so that he's thinking of changing the name of the cafe. All the food is home-made and the menu is adaptable.

Vegetarian Bolognese - £3.50, Stir Fry with Rice (V) - £3.50, Stroganoff with Rice - £3.75, Veggie Burger with Chips & Peas - £3.45, Various Cakes 99p, 2 Veggie Sausages, Chips & Beans - £2.75
*Opening Hours*
*Monday - Wednesday: 8am-5.30pm*
*Thursday - Saturday: 8am-5.30pm (-9pm in summer)*
*Sunday: 8am-3pm*

## HOVE

### Ashoka (Restaurant)

95/97 Church Road
Hove      01273 734193

**Type of Cuisine:** Indian/English

**Breakdown:** (out of 100 dishes) **Vegetarian:** 25%; **Vegan:** 0%

A truly authentic tandoori restaurant. The blend of Indian food and music make for a spicy sensory experience. Ashoka was voted 'Indian Restaurant of the Year' by the Daily Mirror in 1995. The choice of vegetarian dishes is limited but high quality, so if you're the indecisive type then this one could be for you. Not much on offer for vegans - a few side dishes perhaps.

Vegetable Biriany - £5.55,  Mixed Vegetable Rogan - £3.95, Garlic Naan - £1.75, Sunday Buffet (12noon-3pm) - £6.95 (adult) & £3.95 (under14's)
*Opening Hours*
*Every day: Noon - 3pm & 6pm - Midnight*
**Additional**
**Music:** Indian
**Service:** 10% service charge
**Booking:** Necessary

# Frogan's (Restaurant) ❹
117 Western Road
Hove     01273 773586

**Type of Cuisine:** Organic Vegetarian

**Breakdown:** (out of 15 dishes) **Vegetarian:** 100%; **Vegan:** 75%

Fresh fruit and vegetables that haven't been sprayed with pesticides, eggs from rescued hens, and a lack of dead animals on the premises - heaven! Boasting Sussex's one and only vegan organic Sunday roast, Frogan's has lovely food and is delightfully friendly. Ethical eating for a truly clear conscience is the order of the day at this restaurant.

Egg Plant Parmigian - £3.95 (lunch) / £7.95 (dinner), Coconut Bean Feast (V) - £3.95 (lunch) / £6.95 (dinner), Freshly Squeezed Organic

Juices, Vegan Ice-creams, Full Veggie/Vegan Breakfasts

*Opening Hours*
Sunday & Monday: 10am-5pm                    *Tuesday: CLOSED*
*Wednesday - Saturday:10am-5pm/ 7pm-10pm*
**Additional**
**Service:** Lunch at own discretion/Dinner 10% added to bill
**Booking:** Usually necessary for evening meals
**Organic:** 80%- 90% organic

# Ipanema (Restaurant)

**121 Western Road**
**Hove      01273 779474**

**Type of Cuisine:** Greek and Spanish

**Breakdown:** (out of 200 dishes) **Vegetarian:** 10%; **Vegan:** 0%

Ipanema says: "When you're in a Mediterranean country on holiday the food tastes great. It's not just the flavours, it's the atmosphere and you can find all these at Ipanema restaurant in Hove." The food is freshly prepared and it's based on traditional home-made recipes from Greece and Spain.

Cannelloni Florentina - £4.90, Rigatoni Primavera with Vegetable, Cream & White Wine - £4.50, Vegetarian Stuffed Peppers - £6.20, Patatas Bravas (Deep-Fried Potatoes in a Spicy Sauce) - £2.70

*Opening Hours*
*Monday - Friday: 10.30am - Midnight · Saturday & Sunday: 11am - Midnight*
**Additional**
**Music:** Live romantic tunes and sing-a-long favourites
**Service:** 10% service charge
**Booking:** Necessary on weekends

## Oki-Nami (Restaurant)

208 Church Road
Hove     01273 773777

**Type of Cuisine:** Japanese

**Breakdown:** (out of 98 dishes) **Vegetarian:** 28%; **Vegan:** 21%

Oki-Nami caters for veggies and vegans with a creative menu and
some unusual vegan dishes at very reasonable prices.
Sushi with mushroom or pickled plum - £3, Hijiki (seaweed, noodles
& vegetables) - £2.95, Horenso (spinach in seasame sauce) - £3, Age
Tofu - £2.95
*Opening Times*
*Everyday: 12pm - 2.30pm & 6pm - 10.30pm     Tuesday lunchtime: CLOSED*

## Papadoms Indian (Restaurant)

75 Portland Road
Hove     01273 729602

**Type of Cuisine:** Indian

**Breakdown: Vegetarian:** 25%; **Vegan:** 25%

Eat in, take-away or have your meal delivered - it's all the same
price. There are 20 vegetarian dishes to choose from and they're all
priced between £1.95 and £2.95 so order a few to share.

Vegetable Bhuna - £2.95, Vegetarian Soup - £1.45, Vegetable Jalfry
- £2.95, Dall - £2.75, Sag Aloo - £2.95, Bhindi Bhajee - £2.95
*Opening Hours*
*Sunday - Thursday: Noon - 2pm & 5.30pm - 11.30pm*
*Friday & Saturday: Noon - 2pm & 5.30pm - Midnight*

# The Fortune Cookie (Take-Away)

35 Boundary Road
Hove      01273 418860

**Type of Cuisine:** Chinese

**Breakdown:** (out of 123 dishes) **Vegetarian:** 7%; **Vegan:** 6%

The Fortune Cookie specialises in Szechuan, Cantonese and Peking cuisine and are willing to cook what your heart desires *and* deliver it to your door. The range of vegetarian and vegan delicacies is limited compared to the amount of meat dishes they do. However look closely at the back page of the menu and you will find a few things to delight you.

Vegetarian Spring Roll - £1.50, Mixed Vegetable Chow Mein - £3, Fried Mixed Vegetables with Cashew nuts in Fermented Soya Bean Sauce - £3.10, Sweet & Sour Mixed Vegetables - £2.80, Mushroom Foo Yung - £3

*Opening Hours*
*Monday, Wednesday & Thursday: Noon - 2pm/5pm - 11.30pm*
*Friday & Saturday: Noon - 2pm/5pm - Midnight*
*Sunday: 5pm - 11.30pm*

# The Sanctuary (Cafe/Bar)   **8**

51-55 Brunswick Street East
Hove      01273 770002

**Type of Cuisine:** Global Vegetarian

**Breakdown:** (out of 40 dishes) **Vegetarian:** 100%; **Vegan:** 30%

The Sanctuary is totally groovy. The sassy lime greens, oranges and blues that surround you while you lounge on the sofa upstairs supping cappuccino can make even the most geeky of people feel totally with it - I know! A meat-free menu - hooray! The blackboard has five main dishes which change daily and the standard is consistently high. There's usually at least one vegan option on there and the soup is always vegan.

Moroccan Vegetable Stew with Basmati Rice (V) - £5.25, Spinach & Thai Spice Soup with bread (V) - £2.45, Vegetables Sauteed in coconut, chilli, corriander & brandy - £5.25

*Opening Hours*
*Monday: Noon - 11.30pm*        *Tuesday - Sunday: 10am - 11.30pm*

**Additional**
**Music:** Funky jazzy soul tunes and the odd bit of techno

# The Spanish Connection (Restaurant)

**38 Waterloo Street**
**Hove**              **01273 747555**
tapashouse@aol.com

**Type of Cuisine:** Spanish Tapas

**Breakdown:** (out of 30+ dishes) **Vegetarian:** 35%; **Vegan:** 33%

Spanish Connection offers a selection of 11 vegetarian dishes plus daily specials. If you want something a bit different go here and experience a bit of Spain even if it's cold and raining in Brighton!

Patata Brava - £2.50 or Tortilla Espanola - £2.50, Earbanzos Con Espinancas (V) - £2.75, Pisto (Stewed Summer Vegetables) - £2.95, Berenjenas Fritas (Deep-Fried Battered Aubergine) - £2.75
*Opening Hours*
*Tuesday - Saturday: 7pm - late*

**Additional**
**Music:** Spanish
**Service:** Left to the customer or 10% with 8 or more people
**Booking:** Necessary - especially Friday and Saturday

# ROTTINGDEAN

## Champagne House (Restaurant)
14 Nevill Road
Rottingdean
Brighton          01273 307585

**Type of Cuisine:** Chinese

**Breakdown:** (out of 121 dishes) **Vegetarian:** 10%; **Vegan:** 5%

A few good veggie options at reasonable prices.

Vegetarian Singapore Noodles - £4.50, Vegetarian Spring Roll -
£2.60, Seaweed (V) - £3.50

*Opening Hours*
*Monday: Noon - 2pm & 6pm - 11.30*
*Tuesday: 6pm - 11.30pm*
*Wednesday - Saturday: Noon - 2pm & 6pm - 11.30pm*

**Additional**
**Music:** Oriental
**Service:** 10% charge
**Booking:** Necessary on Saturdays

## The Olde Cottage (Cafe)

62 High Street
Rottingdean
Brighton          01273 303426

**Type of Cuisine:** English

**Breakdown:** (out of 20 dishes) **Vegetarian:** 50%; **Vegan:** 10%

The Olde Cottage is really old! It was built in 1589AD and has three olde worlde dining rooms. There is also a large tea garden where you can while away those lazy summer afternoons. There are vegetarian dishes and a few basic vegan ones to choose from.

Vegetarian Quiche of the Day - £5, Mushroom & Tomato
Toastie (V) £2
*Opening Hours*
*Monday & Tuesday: CLOSED*
*Wednesday - Sunday: Noon - 8pm*

# BRIGHTON SHOPS

## Blackout

53 Kensington Place
Brighton          01273 671741

Fabulously Funky Things!

Beautifully hand crafted bags, clothes, beads and bobbles and some amazing incense decorate this den of delight. The cards are very unusual, recycled and right on. Goods are from all over the planet - discovered by an environmentally conscious collective. Blackout is well worth a visit.

**Enviro:** Carrier Bags are made from recycled paper, waste is recycled and recycled stationery is used. The 'Blackout' products are made by women's co-operatives and are fair trade.

*Opening times*
*Monday - Saturday: 10am - 6pm*

## Evolution
**161 North Street**
**Brighton**          **01273 205379**

Gift Shop. Evolution is a Buddhist Right Livelihood Business. They aim to help Buddhists to work together and all profits go to charitable projects in Britain and abroad. They sell candles, household items, books, cards, essential oils and many other goodies. Evolution shops can be found dotted around the country

and each one is a treasure chest of fasinating bits and bobs.
Brighton has the luxury of two Evolution shops, both are
delightful.

**Cruelty-free:** This branch says it attempts to ensure that all
products are produced without cruelty to animals.
**Enviro:** All used cardboard and packaging is recycled and they
encourage customers to re-use bags. Aims to ensure that all goods
are environmentally sound and that producers are paid a fair price
for their work.
*Opening Hours*
*Monday - Saturday: 10am - 5.30pm        Sunday: Noon - 5.30pm*

# Evolution
**89 Western Road**
**Brighton           01273 727123**

Gift shop. This shop provides friendly service. They sell cards, gifts,
futons, unusual furniture, fake fur stuff, candles and non-leather
products.
Overseas sources are checked to ensure fair trade.
**Cruelty-free:** This branch says it does not sell any products of
animal origin.
**Enviro:**  Cardboard is recycled locally. All tins, glass, paper and
plastic is recycled.

*Opening Hours*
*Monday - Saturday: 10am - 5.30pm        Sunday: 11am - 5pm*

# Evolution Arts & Health Centre
**2 Silwood Terrace**
**Brighton           01273 729803**
**evolutionarts@compuserve.com**

Alternative arts and health education centre and natural
health clinic run by a team of Buddhists who are all vegetarian.
They offer an extensive range of treatments and classes and
sometimes weekend or day courses focusing on a particular craft or

therapy. Classes, courses and workshops are in drawing, mosaic, pottery, dance, creative writing, singing, taichi, massage, dramatherapy and meditation.

*Opening Hours*
*Monday - Friday: 10am - 1.30pm*

## Health Link
**21f Station Road**
**Portslade**
**Brighton**          **01273 420120**

High Street Health Shop

Healthlink is an independent health shop with qualified product advisors. They specialise in vegetarian and vegan foods, organic foods, vitamin & mineral supplements, herbal & homeopathic remedies and cruelty-free cosmetics.

**Cruelty-free:** Beauty Without Cruelty products etc.
**Enviro:** Recycle waste, re-use carrier bags and use recycled stationery.
*Opening Hours*
*Monday - Saturday: 9am - 5.30pm*

## Hocus Pocus
**38 Gardner Street**
**Brighton**          **01273 572202**

A very different kind of shop - A "Creative Lifestyle Shop" encouraging the work of quality crafts people.

Hocus Pocus is relatively new to Brighton and is very popular - no doubt partly due to the positive attitude of the two women who run the shop. Hocus Pocus has managed to slip into the gap between hippydom and super cool - it is New Age and Alternative selling Tarot cards, crystals, grain incenses, legal highs and daily tarot consultations. A huge range of products are available here from angelic artefacts to alien lifeforms and aromatherapy.

*Opening Hours*
*Monday - Saturday: 9am - 7.30pm (May -Sept) 10am - 6pm (Oct- April)*
*Sunday: 11am - 6pm (May -Sept) 12am - 4.30pm (Oct- April)*

# Infinity Foods Cooperative

**25 North Road**
**Brighton**      **01273 603563**

Central Brighton's excellent wholefood shop specialises in
vegetarian, vegan and organic foods - including fruit & veg, pulses,
herbs, pates and much more. Also has its own bakery and sells a
wide variety of breads and lunch time treats - sandwiches, rolls,
pasties. Offers refilling  service for all sorts of products - apple
juice, toilet cleaner, laundry liquid, tamari etc. Money saving large
sizes available.
Retailers/trade can order products in bulk direct from **Infinity
Foods Wholesale** - contact the warehouse at: 67 Norway Street,
Portslade; **tel: 01273 424060**.
**Cruelty-free:** Specialise in vegan, vegetarian and organic produce.
**Enviro:** Recycle all paper and cardboard.

*Opening Hours*
*Monday - Thursday & Saturday: 9.30am - 5.30pm    Friday: 9.30am - 6pm*

# Sunny Foods

**76 Beaconsfield Road**
**Brighton**      **01273 507879**

Animal and people friendly! Sunny Foods promotes vegan and
organic foods and endeavours to keep its prices low.

Products include health foods, organic fruit and vegetables, organic
foods and vegan specialities. The shop is quite a way out from the
central shopping area of Brighton, but it's the best thing since
sliced bread for the people who live around Preston Park.

*to Vegetarian Brighton*                                    **119**

**Cruelty-free:** Specialises in vegan and organic foods - everything from garlic coleslaw and vegetable pastas to Tofutti ice cream.
**Enviro:** Recycle whenever possible and sell no genetically modified products.

*Opening Hours*
*Every Day: 8am - 8pm*

## The Peace and Environment Centre

**Gardner Street**
**Brighton**       **01273 692880**
**bripeace@pavillion.co.uk**

Ethical trade shop with a library and educational unit.

The Peace and Environment Centre is run entirely by volunteers who work really hard. For ethical pressies, this is the place. It sells T-shirts - including a Viva! range, stationery, books, journals, cards, crafts and gifts from organisations working for peace, justice and environmental protection.

**Cruelty-free:** Sell Viva! products and a variety of vegetarian and vegan books.

**Enviro:** Recycles packaging etc. and fund raises for environmental organisations.

*Opening Hours*
*Monday - Saturday: 10am - 5.30pm*  *Sunday: CLOSED*

## Tucan

**29 Bond Street**
**Brighton**  **01273 326351**

Fair Trade Shop with Latin America.

Tucan has a wide range of authentic exotic artefacts for that special gift. They specialise in furniture and crafts, clothing and jewellery.
*Opening Hours*
*Monday - Saturday: 9.30am - 6pm*
*Sunday: CLOSED*

# Vegetarian Shoes

12 Gardner Street
North Laines
Brighton          01273 691913
http.//www.vegetarian-shoes.co.uk

Vegetarian Shoes, Jackets and Accessories.

Vegetarian Shoes sells wait for it... vegetarian shoes among other things. If you haven't already ordered from them by mail then pop in and choose from a large selection of ethical wares. Whether you're after dainty court shoes or knee length biker boots you'll find them here and they're top quality. I've had a pair of vegan biker boots for over four years now and they still look as good as new.

**Cruelty-free:** Yes. (Sells vegan shoes, boots, jackets, bags, T shirts, belts, wallets.)
**Enviro:** Recycles cardboard packaging.

*Opening Hours*
*Monday - Saturday: 10am - 5.30pm*

# Winfalcon Healing Centre & Shop

28-29 Ship Street
Brighton          01273 728997
winfalcon@dial.pipex.com

Complementary therapies, readings, channelling, natural remedies, aura imaging, holistic shop, crystals.

If you have come to Brighton for the New Age healing vibes (man!) then head for Winfalcon's for your fix. They can provide all sorts of remedies and therapies - and not just for you - take along your companion animal too. A relaxing and enjoyable Aladdin's cave with friendly staff.

**Cruelty-free:** Nothing is tested on animals. Sells Aloe Vera products, flower remedies, crystals etc.

**Enviro:** Recycle paper where possible, re-use bags and boxes. Use recycled products where possible.

*Opening Hours*
*Monday - Friday: 10am - 5.30pm*
*Saturday: 10am - 6pm*
*Sunday: Noon - 4pm*

# LEWES

### The Garden Room (Cafe)
**14 Station Street**
**Lewes**          **01273 844855**

**Type of Cuisine:** Cakes & Snacks

**Breakdown: Vegetarian:** 95%; **Vegan:** 0%

The Garden Room is available for party booking in the evenings (minimum number 6) and they have regular exibitions of paintings. They serve cream teas and a range of home-made cakes as well as a wide range of vegetarian tasty dishes.

Nut Loaf with Apricot Sauce - £3.80, Spinach & Mushroom Roulade - £3.80, Savory Pancake Gateaux - £3.80, Jacket Potatoes with Various Fillings

*Opening Hours*
*Monday - Saturday: 10am - 5.30pm*

# Shanaz Tandoori & Balti Restaurant

83 High Street
Lewes                01273 4880838

**Type of Cuisine:** Indian

**Breakdown: Vegetarian:** 25%; **Vegan:** 0%

Spice up your life at Shanaz! They adapt their specialities for vegetarians; however it's no-go for vegans.

Indian Garlic Mushrooms - £2.90, Vegetable Samosa - £2.50, Vegetable-Stuffed Nan - £1.50, Aloo Gobi - £3.25, Tarka Dall - £3.25
*Opening Hours*
*Every day: Noon - 2.30pm & 6pm - 12.30am*

# Seasons of Lewes (Cafe)                ❼

199 High Street
Lewes                01273 473968

**Type of Cuisine:** Vegetarian

**Breakdown: Vegetarian:** 100%; **Vegan:** 60%

Refreshing to see a cafe so committed to vegetarianism, organic produce and value for money. Their slogan is "Seasons - Food For People Who Care About What They Eat" and this mother and daughter team obviously care about what they cook.

Organic Pumpkin & Ginger Soup with Wholemeal Bread (V) - £2.30, Brazil & Cashew Roast with Tomato & Herb Sauce (V) - £3.95,

Butterbean & Cider Casserole with Organic Brown Rice (V) - £3.95,
Leek & Mushroom Pie (V) - £3.95, Coffee & Walnut Cake - £1
*Opening Hours*
*Tuesday - Saturday: 9.30am - 5.30pm*

# *Seasons*
### Vegetarian Cafe & Tea Room
*199 High Street, Lewes*
*East Sussex BN7 2NS*
*Tel: 01273 473968*

*Also Outside Catering*
*Everything Homemade*

## LEWES SHOPS

## Landsdown Health Foods
**44 Cliffe High Street**
**Lewes** 01273 474681

Health food shop

Sells a wide range of organic and wholefoods as well as herbal
remedies, cosmetics, books and household goods. Operates with
ethical principles and offers helpful, qualified advice.

**Cruelty-free:** Yes - specialises in veggie foods and
cruelty-free cosmetics
**Enviro:** Re-use carrier bags, ask before giving bags away and use
all environmentally friendly cleaning products.
*Opening Hours*
*Monday - Saturday: 9am - 5.30pm*

## Full Of Beans

**96-97 High Street**
**Lewes**          **01273 472627**

Wholefood shop

Established in 1978 by Sarah and John, they manufacture their own tofu, tempeh and miso from organic soya beans and provide a large range of organic dairy and sheep products as well as special diet products. They also do an organic vegetable box scheme.

**Cruelty-free:** Specialises in vegetarian foods.
**Enviro:** Accept carrier bags for re-use and recycle egg boxes.

*Opening Hours    Monday - Saturday: 9am - 5.30pm*

# WORTHING

## Seasons Wholefood Restaurant  ⑦ᵇ

**15 Crescent Road**
**Worthing**          **01903 236011**

**Type of Cuisine:** Vegetarian English and popular foreign dishes

**Breakdown:** (out of 10 dishes) **Vegetarian:** 100%; **Vegan:** 50%

Seasons offers a high standard of vegetarian and vegan food. Well worth a visit if you're in the area.

Mousakka - £3.50, Carrot & Courgette Layer - £3.50, Brazil Nut Shepherds Pie (V) - £3.50, Vegetable Curry (V) - £3.50, Soup of the Day - £1.50, Small Fresh Salad - £1.40
*Opening Hours*
*Monday - Saturday: 9am - 3pm*

# NATIONAL CHAINS

## The Body Shop

**41/43 North Street, Brighton**     **01273 327048**
*Opening Hours     Monday - Saturday: 9am - 6pm   Sunday: 11am - 5pm*

**22 George Street, Hove**     **01273 724481**
*Opening Hours     Monday - Saturday: 9am - 5.30pm*

**80 Montague Street, Worthing**     **01903 214369**
*Opening Hours     Monday - Saturday: 9am - 5.30pm*

Huge range of toiletries and cosmetics; against animal testing and many products are vegan.

## Holland & Barrett

**105 London Road, Brighton**     **01273 696209**
**66-68 North Street, Brighton**     **01273 746343**
*Opening Hours     Monday - Saturday: 9am - 5.30pm*

**68 George Street, Hove**     **01273 321873**
*Opening Hours     Monday - Saturday: 9am - 5.30pm*

**11 Warwick Street, Worthing**     **01903 231274**
*Opening Hours     Monday - Saturday: 9am - 5.30pm*

Health food shops selling a wide range of vegetarian and vegan foods, toiletries and supplements.

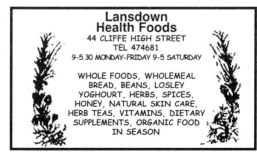

**Lansdown Health Foods**
44 CLIFFE HIGH STREET
TEL 474681
9-5.30 MONDAY-FRIDAY 9-5 SATURDAY

WHOLE FOODS, WHOLEMEAL BREAD, BEANS, LOSLEY YOGHOURT, HERBS, SPICES, HONEY, NATURAL SKIN CARE, HERB TEAS, VITAMINS, DIETARY SUPPLEMENTS, ORGANIC FOOD IN SEASON

# Index

*to Vegetarian Brighton*

## SHOPS

## USEFUL PHONE NUMBERS

**Viva!: 01273 777688**
**Tourist Information: 01273 292599**
**or call in at Bartholomew Square, Brighton**
**Local Weather Forecast: 01839 400177**

## Travel

**Taxis: 01273 202020**
**(There is a taxi rank at the rail station.)**
**British Rail: 0345 484950**
**National Express Coaches: 01273 886200 or 700406**
**By road: Brighton is approx. 60 miles via A23/M23**
**from London.**

# If you don't want these little piggies to go to market...

Join ***Viva!***

Every year in Britain, more than 700 million animals face the barbarity of slaughter - many fully conscious. Most spend their short lives in confinement, pain and misery.

Every year the earth staggers closer to environmental disaster. Whether polluted water or torched forests; eroded topsoil or spreading deserts - livestock production is at the heart of the problem. Meanwhile, the oceans are dying from the constant rape of overfishing.

Every year, millions of people in the developing world die from hunger - alongside fields of fodder destined for the West's livestock.

Every year, proof increases that vegetarians are healthier than meat eaters. Yet the meat industry is subsidised by the tax payer; even when it creates diseases such as BSE. Overnight, with the simple decision to stop eating meat and fish, you cease to play a part in this insanity.

## Why Viva!?

Viva! is the only vegetarian and vegan charity in the UK dedicated to campaigning on the animals' behalf. With regular hard-hitting campaigns, *Viva!* keeps the debate open and the information flowing.

Viva! is also investing in the future. With a huge commitment to youth education, Viva! is sowing the seeds of a more compassionate tomorrow.

Viva! helps people change to a vegetarian or vegan diet.

Viva! needs your help and support to end the shame of animal suffering.

## Join us...

"I wouldn't want to kill animals and I don't want them killed on my behalf. I wish Viva! every success with its vital campaigns."

**Joanna Lumley, actress**

"I am honoured to be a Founder of a charity with such fine aims. I fully support Viva! and hope you will too."

**Pam Ferris, actress**

# The campaign trail...

Viva! has launched many successful campaigns since its birth in 1994. A few examples are:

### Babe
Campaign against pig farming which

coincided with the film and produced more than 150 news stories. Viva! local groups distributed 150,000 leaflets in just one week and caused pork/bacon consumption to drop by 10% nationwide.

### Don't bury your head...
Viva! leads the campaign against 'exotic' meats and persuaded Tesco, Somerfield and Booker to withdraw from the trade.

### Going for the kill
Major new and ongoing campaign to expose the myth behind humane slaughter.

### You'd be mad to eat beef
Included the BSE Helpline, which took calls from thousands of meat eaters and helped them go vegetarian. It was Viva! who first raised the gelatine and beef derivatives concerns.

### The Silent Ark & Livewire Guide to Going, Being &Staying Veggie
Launch of two books which bring together the vegetarian issues. Serialised in the Times.

### SCOFF!
Schools' Campaign Opposed to Factory Farming
Major new teen campaign.

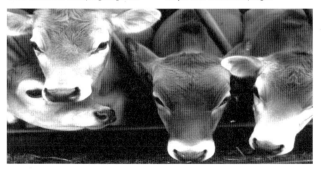

# Join Viva!...

## Choose your category

### Supporter (£12)
Supporters receive a free issue of Viva!Life every quarter, packed with info on our campaigns, ideas on how you can help and the latest news - also a car sticker, posters and pack. Make a donation of £5 or more in addition to your subs and receive a special certificate.

### Campaigner (£29.90)
Campaigners receive Viva!Life, car sticker, posters - plus an exclusive T-shirt, Campaigner's mug and copy of the classic book, the Silent Ark.

### Activist (£4.99; under 18's)
Activists receive their own mini-mag, Vivactive! every quarter - packed with penpals, poems, letters and gossip! Also posters and stickers.

## Campaigning for animals Fighting for change

❑ **YES**, please send me a free **Viva!** pack

❑ **YES**, I'd like to join **Viva!** and enclose £12 ❑ (adult supporter);
£29.90 ❑ (adult campaigner) **OR** £4.99 ❑ (under 18's only)

❑ **YES**, I'd like to make a donation to help animals and enclose:
£5 ❑  £10 ❑  £20 ❑  £30 ❑  £100 ❑  Other ❑ £............

I enclose a cheque/PO payable to Viva! or please debit my CAF/Switch/credit card:

Expiry date:................................ Signature on Card................................................

Title:.................. First name:........................... Surname:................................

Address:........................................................... Tel: (home)...............................

.......................................................................... Tel: (work)................................

Postcode:............................................ Date of Birth (if under 18)........................

Registered charity 1037486

**Return to: Viva!, 12 Queen Square, Brighton BN1 3FD**